OPERATION GREYLORD: BROCTON LOCKWOOD'S STORY

BY BROCTON LOCKWOOD

WITH HARLAN H. MENDENHALL

WITH A FOREWORD BY PETER M. MANIKAS

Southern Illinois University Press / Carbondale and Edwardsville

Printed in the United States of America

Edited by Mara Lou Hawse

Designed by David Ford

Production supervised by Natalia Nadraga

Library of Congress Cataloging-in-Publication Data

Lockwood, Brocton.
   Operation Greylord: Brocton Lockwood's Story.
    1. Lockwood, Brocton.   2. Judges—Illinois—Cook County—Biography.
3. Judicial corruption—Illinois—Cook County.   4. Justice, Administration
of—Illinois—Cook County.   I. Mendenhall, Harlan H.   II. Title.
KF373.L545A3   1989   345.73'0234   89–6022
ISBN 0–8093–1545–9   347.305234

The paper used in this publication meets the minimum requirements of
American National Standard for Information Sciences
—Permanence of Paper for Printed Library Materials, ANSI Z39.48-1984. ∞

to Jessica and Kathy

whose love sustained me

through many lonely and frightening weeks

Contents

Foreword

Peter M. Manikas

Executive Director

Special Commission on the Administration of Justice in
    Cook County

As this is being written, it has been more than four years since
the Greylord prosecutions began. So far, seventy persons—eleven
judges, thirty-eight lawyers, seven police officers, ten deputy
sheriffs, three deputy clerks, and a court-appointed receiver—have
been convicted of federal crimes. And the Greylord investigation
continues.

In response to the first Greylord convictions, the chief judge of
Cook County's court, Harry G. Comerford, appointed a blue ribbon
commission in August 1984. The principal mission of this forty-
three member panel was to make recommendations to the court to
prevent Greylord-type misconduct from recurring.

The blue ribbon reform panel was formally called the Special Commission on the Administration of Justice in Cook County. However, it
quickly became known as the Solovy Commission, after its chairman Jerold S. Solovy, a prominent lawyer from one of Chicago's most
prestigious law firms.

The Solovy Commission has taken a broad view of its mandate and
has made almost two hundred recommendations to the court and to
other agencies as well. It is too early to tell what will ultimately result
from the Solovy Commission's work. But some changes already have
occurred and there is momentum for further reform.

As a result of the Solovy Commission's proposals:

1. The Illinois Supreme Court enacted a strong rule requiring judges to
   disclose their financial holdings. Illinois now has the nation's most
   stringent financial disclosure rule for judges.

2. More cases are now randomly assigned. It is more difficult for corrupt
   lawyers to maneuver their cases to get them before a "friendly" judge.

3. Steps are being taken to remove the processing of parking tickets from Chicago's traffic court. The fixing of parking tickets—for favors and for a price—has been a perennial problem and leads to more serious corruption.

4. New merit procedures are used for appointing high-ranking court officials—such as the county's chief probation officer and the public defender. In the past, these departments were widely considered to be havens for political patronage workers.

5. In Chicago's branch courts, where minor criminal cases are heard, reforms have been enacted to prevent case hustling by unscrupulous lawyers. In addition, court personnel are rotated between courtrooms to prevent the formation of corrupt cliques of courtroom employees.

Much remains to be done. Circuit court judges, for example, are still selected through a political process that emphasizes party loyalty and ignores judicial competence. Too often, lawyers are slated for judicial office because of the favors they have performed for party leaders. Once they are elected, all too often the favors continue. To prevent future Greylords, we must insulate the selection of judges from the political system.

In addition, professional disciplinary agencies must develop more effective strategies for investigating court-related misconduct. The crimes that occurred in Cook County's courts persisted over a period of decades. The corruption endured and became entrenched because corrupt lawyers and judges knew there was little risk their crimes would be reported.

Perhaps lawyers fail to report misconduct because they fear retaliation, or because they do not want to be considered whistle-blowers, or because they view the professional disciplinary agencies as ineffective. In any case, this failure has serious repercussions because the legal profession's regulatory agencies largely rely on lawyers and others to bring complaints.

Brocton Lockwood, of course, was one of the few exceptions. He had the courage and conviction to come forward, but the price he paid has been high. Judge Lockwood's account of Greylord not only informs us about public corruption it inspires us as well. The public owes Judge Lockwood a debt of gratitude that cannot easily be repaid.

Preface

I have been called a white knight. I have been called a Judas in black robes. Some say I'm a whistle-blower and others describe me as an idealist or a do-gooder. I am none of these—neither a hero nor a crusader. I am a proud member of a profession that's frequently criticized and often maligned—but which I believe is the cornerstone of the democratic system. Perhaps I'm part of a dying breed; I am a trial lawyer.

When I first became aware of the extent of the corruption poisoning my state's judiciary, I felt cheated of my inheritance. The court system, where I had been trained to perform, was being bought and sold by bagmen and politicians. Trial lawyers were almost extinct. That scared me. It also made me so damned angry that I wanted to do something to change the situation—something that would give me back a sense of pride in my profession.

I grew up in two worlds. One world was the academic environment of Southern Illinois University where I mingled with the faculty colleagues of my mother who was a business education professor there. The other world was my grandfather's farm, in a region of Illinois known for its old-style fundamentalism and straight-arrow Americanism. It is a world in which there are only two kinds of people—the good guys and the bad guys. There is right and there is wrong, and a person quickly learns the difference.

My parents divorced when I was very young, and most of my growing up was done at the side of my grandfather. It was he who taught me the moral concepts that became the foundation for my life. Some say I am old-fashioned—one hundred years behind my time—in my ideas of right and wrong. That's not true. I'm not a fundamentalist—I don't even go to church. I just grew up with people who were and who did.

I had been a trial lawyer for nine years when in 1978, at the age of thirty-three, I was appointed an associate circuit court judge in

Marion, Illinois, located in the southern part of the state. I soon learned that the judges in southern Illinois were expected to serve a six-week stint each year in Chicago, to reduce the backlog in the Cook County system. There, I worked in the housing court first, then in the traffic court. It was in the traffic court that I began to observe and to feel the effects of the official corruption that ran rampant. The discovery was no great credit to my intelligence; a blind person could have seen what was going on. Bribery was an open, established practice, ruled by bagmen. Perhaps I was naive, but I was shocked. Decisions were bought and sold like commodity futures.

I deeply believe that without an honest, open, independent judicial system our democracy will eventually fail. The judiciary, home of the jury system, serves to mediate our social differences in a fair fashion; it does not simply serve the powerful. The Chicago judicial system, on the other hand, served only the Chicago political machine and the power brokers.

My anger was soon focused on the epitome of corruption—Judge Richard F. LeFevour, presiding judge in the Chicago traffic court. Judge LeFevour seemed to threaten everything I valued in the system, and he offended me personally. At that time, LeFevour challenged me to stop him. He was raw power—and I was nobody. As far as he was concerned, I was no threat. That drove me to accept the challenge. I started to consider my "get even" options.

Months later, I had discovered five other persons on the Chicago legal scene who hated the corruption in the judiciary as much as I did. We tentatively joined forces and the battle was on. Within three years, seventy officials had joined the ranks of those we successfully prosecuted. At this writing, five years have passed, the statute of limitations has run, but the battle continues.

I wish to pay tribute here to those five men who first shared my ideals, designed a counteroffensive to corruption, and, more importantly, put their careers on the line to preserve our judicial system. Names and official titles of our team members, at that particular time, follow: William Megary, FBI agent; Dan Reidy, assistant U.S. attorney; David V. Ries, undercover FBI agent; Charles "Chuck" Sklarsky, assistant U.S. attorney, and Dan Webb, U.S. attorney, Northern District of Illinois.

It was not until my involvement in this vicious battle ended that I decided to go public with the story of what had happened. All events, dates, and places in this story of the FBI investigation, tagged Operation Greylord, are as accurate as my memory allows. Except for a few persons who have not been convicted of criminal misconduct, all names used are the actual names of those involved. The first time a pseudonym is used in this book, it is identified in a footnote for the reader's information.

Because I believe that this is an important story and should be told, I obtained the assistance of the most competent writer in the southern Illinois area—my friend, Harlan H. Mendenhall, retired journalism teacher and long-time professional writer, from Southern Illinois University. It is my sincere desire that our collective efforts will help to bring about a revitalized court system.

Operation Greylord: Brocton Lockwood's Story

BLACKWOOD: Tony will be on the bench pretty
soon.

WINSTON: But why would he want to?

BLACKWOOD: Well, after he stole enough money . . .

1

Monkey in a Robe

My first judicial assignment in Chicago came eight months after my
appointment to the bench. I felt like the new kid on the block. It was
still uncomfortable to exercise the awesome power of the position.

Although I had spent nine years as a trial lawyer, that courtroom
experience had not prepared me to accept the responsibility for making ultimate decisions. Probably my stint as a policeman settling
disputes on the street was more helpful. But the whole experience
was new to me, and I was afraid of making mistakes. It was not until
later that I realized no decision can be perfect. Before I went to Chicago, I still expected to achieve perfection in my own decision-mak-
ing processes.

It may seem odd that I was assigned to Chicago. My home and my
regular assignment were in Marion, Illinois, 350 miles south of the
city. The southern nine counties in Illinois make up the first judicial
circuit, which includes Marion.

Years ago, the Chicago court system began borrowing judges from
the downstate counties to help with a backlog in the Cook County
system. By 1978, annual assignments were given to each of the
downstate circuits and, at that time, the first judicial circuit was
required to provide forty-two judge weeks a year. Before I was appointed, I was aware I would have to spend up to six weeks annually in
Chicago, helping fulfill our circuit's allotment. I knew that the assignments were generally broken down into two-week intervals, a lot
of time to spend away from home—and the farm—but it seemed like a
good opportunity to enjoy some time in the city.

In retrospect, my expectations about my initial city assignment were erroneous. For one thing, I had fully anticipated having to work hard, long days. After all, downstate judges were going to Chicago to relieve a backlog that had existed for years. It didn't make economic sense for the state to bear the cost of sending judges 350 miles from home to work if it was not going to maximize the workload once they got there.

But my first day at work was a surprise. Downstate, judges started work around 8:00 A.M.; I assumed that would be expected in Chicago. However, there was no one at Chief Judge John Boyle's office when I arrived just after eight o'clock. I checked my official notice from the Supreme Court to make sure I was at the right place. It was nine o'clock before anyone showed up to open the chief judge's office. By then, about ten downstate judges were there, waiting for their assignments. We were ushered into a large waiting area where a secretary asked us to be seated. That rather aloof, self-important, but, I'm sure, very efficient secretary busied herself straightening her desk before she gave us our assignments.

While we waited patiently, one of the judges had a heart attack. We all just watched as the elderly gentleman clutched his chest in pain. The secretary calmly dialed the fire department number for an ambulance. Getting no response, she continued with business as usual. "Let's just go ahead and get our assignments, gentlemen; I'm sure we'll get some assistance for Judge Paulen* in just a very few minutes. As I call your name, I want you to come forward and I will give you your room assignment."

I wanted to do something to help, but for some reason I just sat there like everyone else. It was a bizarre situation.

The secretary proceeded coldly. "Now, let's see. Do we have a Judge Fox?"

A tall, sandy-headed gentleman answered, "Present."

"Judge Fox, you are to go to Room 1301." The secretary drew out the assignment as if it were significant. "Judge Lockwood." "Yes." I responded absent-mindedly, watching the stricken judge and wondering if we were all going to sit there and wait for the man to die.

"Judge Lockwood, we are going to send you . . . to Room 1301."

*Pseudonym.

By the time I got to the elevator, Judge Fox had the door open, and I rushed to catch up. We hurried downstairs to our new assignments where, we hoped, we could regain some semblance of reality.

What a grotesque introduction to the Chicago courts! The general reaction to Judge Paulen's heart attack should have warned me how different things were going to be here. Although I was told later that he did survive and was sent home, no one seemed to care much, one way or the other, what happened to that judge. Where I come from, if one of the four sitting judges in the county had a heart attack, I'm sure business throughout the whole courthouse would come to a screeching halt.

With the obvious exception of Judge Paulen, all of us downstate judges were assigned to the same place—Judge Horan's chambers. Despite that, the secretary called out our names one at a time, and as we came forward she told each of us to go to the same room. The incident reminded me of the Queen's Court in *Alice in Wonderland*.

It was 9:30 A.M. before Judge Horan arrived. He was a sixty-year-old man who didn't look much like a judge. Of course, I'm not sure what judges are supposed to look like, but I always think they should have white hair—and a lot of it. Judge Horan's hair was dark and thinning. He was a little overweight, but his face still had a hawkish appearance. He hurried through an obviously well-rehearsed speech about our importance to the overworked Chicago court system. Then he told the first group of three or four judges that their assignment was, perhaps, the most important in the system—traffic court. They were going right into the trenches as the "first line of defense" against chaos. As soon as those judges walked out, Judge Horan turned to the rest of us and said,"Now, I've got *good* assignments for the rest of you."

Everyone laughed.

Judge Warren Fox from Waukegan and I were sent to the housing court division. I had no idea what the assignment would entail and had no particular feelings about it. Judge Fox, on the other hand, was disturbed. He had volunteered to take some extra time in Chicago with the understanding he would be assigned to divorce court where he could learn how major cases were handled in the Cook County system.

Both of us were new associate circuit judges, unfamiliar with the system. We still thought we were doing something important by coming here to help out the Chicago judges. I expected the assignment to be an educational experience. Downstate, we had always assumed that the best judges and the best lawyers in Illinois were in Chicago. We had been told this for so long that we had come to believe it.

Since everything is so specialized in the city, I thought any assignment would familiarize me in depth with legal problems in that particular area of the law. I was really looking forward to the opportunity to find our how the specialists practiced.

The judges downstate tend to be general practitioners. In Williamson County, I handled everything from traffic cases to major felonies, and from divorces to major civil cases. While I felt that this experience gave me a good overall view of the system, I was sure the specialists would be better informed in their particular areas of the law than I. Judge Fox shared my perception of the city's practice, but neither of us was interested in familiarizing ourselves with the intricacies of a housing court practice.

Chicago's housing court was one of the high-volume courts of the city. Each day it handled thousands of cases dealing with the city's building code violations. The workload in my courtroom—from two hundred to three hundred cases per day—appeared to be overwhelming. But that was before I learned that most of the cases in the judicial system were not actually decided on their merits, as they were downstate.

I was baffled during my first day in housing court. We handled more than 250 cases in an hour and a half—an average of twenty-two seconds per case. On a good day, downstate, I couldn't actually hear a case, even a very small one, in less than about twenty minutes. The system that I encountered was so different that it's difficult to explain.

Every morning, I received ten computer sheets listing twenty-five to thirty-five cases per sheet. Next to the name and number of a case was a space to enter its disposition. Rather than hearing evidence about a case, I simply entered on the appropriate line an abbreviated version of what the prosecutor told me to record.

No defense counsel was present. The defendant usually said nothing. The clerk called a case by saying, "Sheet 4, line 15." I tried to find the right sheet, and the prosecutor said "1–7–79," indicating the date to which the case was continued. Almost all cases were continued for compliance, meaning that they were simply continued over by the prosecutor in the hope that the defendant would tire of coming to court and would repair the code violations. Neither the defendants nor I knew what was going on most of the time. Throughout those two weeks, I never actually understood many of the abbreviations— and I was supposed to be in charge.

Most of the cases were old cases that were continued time after time or dismissed for "substantial compliance" with the ordinance. If a defendant failed to appear, which was not unusual, the prosecution asked for a default judgment of $1,000 per violation and a follow-up date for a motion to vacate judgment. I finally came to understand that in order to move the cases along rapidly, the prosecutor represented both the city and the defendant. The process could be confusing, to say the least, but it was efficient. To me, however, it was a mockery of our system of justice.

On one occasion, I refused to vacate a $14,000 default judgment that had been entered against the defendant, a slum landlord who was in court at least three times a week. In the six or seven years that this particular case had been pending, the landlord had done nothing to correct some major problems. I could see absolutely no reason to grant him leniency and refused to vacate the fine.

The prosecutor, who had stepped up in front of the bench with the slum landlord, stated, "Judge, motion to vacate—next appearance 12–22–79."

"You're telling me that the defendant is making a motion to vacate the judgment, which you don't oppose, and you're asking that this case be rescheduled for December 22. Is that what you're saying counsel?" I asked.

"Yes, that's right Judge. Just set it over. I'm sure the defendant will be able to comply by that time."

I replied, "He has not complied for—what is this—six years now? Is that right? Six years? Is that what you are telling me? I see there is a violation here for fire codes, including no fire escape, etc., and you figure he's going to comply for some reason by the next appearance?"

"We've always had good cooperation from this defendant, your honor. He nearly always shows up," the prosecutor said.

"Your motion will be denied counsel."

There was a pause. Suddenly the defendant exploded.

"What you mean—What you mean?"

Stunned, he turned to the prosecutor. "What he mean?"

As the agitated defendant almost came across the bench, the prosecutor explained that I was not going to vacate the judgment. The prosecutor grabbed the defendant and whispered something to him, to calm him down. They both smiled, thanked me, and left the courtroom. I wondered about the whispers and the smiles. Something funny was going on, for sure.

Later, at the break, I asked my clerk what was going to happen in the case. He laughed and told me that the prosecutor would just bring the case up again next week in front of a cooperative judge who would then vacate the judgment.

"No problem, Judge," the clerk said. "Don't worry about it."

It was all a big joke and nobody worried about it. The whole thing looked like a political deal to me. I found the job in Chicago extremely demeaning, and was very uncomfortable about being involved. If I had had any courage, I would have refused to carry on with the performance. Nothing was being accomplished. My biggest concern was to try to write what the prosecutor said on the appropriate line, and if something was on the wrong line, it really didn't matter much. The disposition of one case was usually the same as it was on all the rest—the cases were continued.

A monkey in a robe could have done the job as well!

I had plenty of free time during that first assignment in Chicago. Supposedly, I was on duty each day until 3:00 P.M. I had been warned by one of the court clerks that I would be checked on by someone, jokingly called "007," who would come around to the chambers about 3:00 P.M. to see if I was there. Once I found I had nothing more to do, however, I refused to wait around. I didn't care whether or not 007 found me in chambers. He could send me home if he wanted to, that would be just fine! As soon as I finished the call for the day, I left. That was usually between 10:30 and 11:00 A.M. Where was all this great backlog of cases I had heard about?

At the end of my first stint in Chicago, 007 actually did show up early one morning. He stopped to let me know that he had dutifully signed me in and out every day, showing that I had stayed in the courthouse until the appropriate departure time. I suppose he thought he was doing me a favor. An insider would have tipped him for his efforts. But I wasn't an insider—at least not yet.

The next time I was sent to Chicago, I caught the traffic court assignment for the first time. It was in the fall of 1979—a cold and rainy time. Inside the building it was just as dreary and depressing. The procedure was the same as before. Everyone collected in Judge Boyle's office. Again, there was one long wait before we were sent down to Judge Horan's office, then another long wait. Finally, I was sent to the traffic court with the first group of judges. I guessed that I was being demoted.

It was 10:00 A.M. by the time I got to Courtroom 1 on the first floor of the traffic court building at 321 North LaSalle Street. Inside, the rooms were dark, dingy, and unattractive, with battered old fold-down seats. The building probably looked pretty much like it had thirty, or forty, or fifty years before. It reminded me of a deteriorating schoolhouse built before the turn of the century. The courtroom and the hallway outside were filled to capacity with angry people, waiting for me.

Three black clerks, a Spanish bailiff, and a middle-aged female prosecutor were all obviously hostile. They acted as if it were my fault I was late. The senior clerk, referred to as the call clerk, informed me that there were 170 defendants for the 9:00 A.M. call and another 150 were milling in the hallway, waiting to come in at 10:30. Then there were two more calls in the afternoon with approximately 350 people.

I shook my head in disbelief!

"You've got to be kidding me," I told the prosecutor.

"I certainly am not kidding you, your honor," she snapped back at me, sounding like a drill sergeant.

I just looked at her. I was tempted to say something, but I controlled myself.

Housing court was one thing, but when it came to judicial mockery, it couldn't hold a candle to traffic court. Six hours! That's 360 minutes to try six hundred cases—about one every thirty seconds.

I turned to the chief call clerk and asked what I was supposed to do. She handed me a booklet and directed me to read the speech. The speech had been prepared for downstate judges by the presiding judge. It told defendants that in traffic court we were concerned about improving defendants' driving habits. It informed them that the city had some of the safest drivers in the world (apparently the presiding judge had never been on the city streets) and that this could be attributed to the fact that the city was more interested in improving driving habits than it was in collecting fines.

I tried to read the speech with a straight face, and when I finished, I asked, "Now what?"

The clerk responded by asking, "How many miles over do you want to hear?"

I was puzzled. "I don't know what you're talking about. What do you mean?"

She looked at me in disgust, as if to say, "How did I get stuck with another greenhorn country judge?"

She explained that the traffic court had produced a fifteen-minute motion picture about traffic safety in Chicago. One punishment was to send traffic violators to watch this movie. I had to decide on the miles over—the cut-off point above the speed limit where this punishment (watching the movie) stopped and fines and convictions began. Judges must decide whether to hear cases over twelve miles, thirteen, fourteen, or whatever.

I said, "Okay, let's do fifteen."

She smiled in relief.

We called the speeders up in groups of ten to twenty. I gave each group a short lecture about slowing down and then sent them to Room 19 where they were "punished" by sitting through the boring fifteen-minute movie.

We moved through the cases quickly. Handling 600 cases a day is one hectic job! Everyone in the system had to work like crazy to put on even a facade of justice. As in housing court, all of the entries were made on computer sheets, with thirty-five or so lines of case names and numbers. And again, it was easy to get on the wrong line. But if I did, what the hell? I was probably going to discharge the case or send the people to the movie anyway. Even so, it was still a lot of work, frantically trying to find the right line and make the appropriate entry in thirty seconds. I felt like I was being punished more than the defendants.

In order to get through the numbers, everything had to be done with the speed of light. Traffic court had developed its own language, rules, and procedures, all aimed at one goal — to save time and get rid of the cases. The drawback to this legal shorthand was that outsiders like myself and, more importantly, the defendants and the public, were excluded from knowing what was going on. Most of the time there was no trial — at least not a real trial. But there were a few exceptions. One stands out in my mind.

The defendant was one of the flashiest black men I have ever seen — obviously accustomed to living life with style and flourish. He was dressed in a white three-piece suit and a frilly, tuxedo shirt trimmed in maroon. His white cape was lined with maroon silk. He sported an oversized white hat with a maroon band, and he wore maroon patent leather shoes with spats.

He was accompanied by two female companions who advertised their profession by wearing elaborate wigs and evening dresses. The two women held the courtroom doors open as the defendant sauntered in, and they struck professional poses on each side of the man as he faced me across the bench.

When asked to remove his hat, the man did so with a flourish and stood stiffly in front of me, as if posing for a seventeenth-century portrait. I picked up the stack of files on my desk. More than one hundred parking tickets had been issued to this man, and they were all in the downtown area. It looked like a long session if the city intended to try every one of these — and I had been told they did, although I had no idea why. The city would expect fines of twenty dollars per ticket, the customary fine at the time.

I turned to the prosecutor, a man named Tommie Kangalos, and asked if he was ready to proceed. He indicated that he was and that the meter maids who had issued the tickets were present. The defendant objected to proceeding at this time because he wanted an attorney appointed to represent him. I explained that attorneys are appointed to represent people only in criminal cases where they face jail terms. Since the city was proceeding on a city ordinance violation, which could be punished only by a fine, he was not entitled to have an attorney appointed.

"Then I want a continuance," the defendant announced in a self-assured manner.

I assumed this had worked before.

"How many times have these cases come up before?" I asked Kangalos.

"Three times, your honor."

"Why do you want a continuance?" I asked the defendant.

"Jes' cause I do," the defendant said, obviously used to getting his way.

In most cases, he would have been right. But his case was a "parking violator," not a "minor mover," so he had more problems than he knew. The city doesn't like parking violators. He remained nonchalant, however, when I denied the request and ordered Kangalos to proceed with his witness, a city meter maid. She testified that the defendant's car had been parked illegally, as described on the first ticket.

I asked the defendant if he had any questions or wanted to make any statements.

"Well, like I was just there for a minute," he responded. "You know, it was no big deal."

"So you're telling me that you were parked illegally for just a minute. Is that what you are saying?" I asked.

"No. Like I was just, well, you know, I was just there a minute." The defendant stopped, unable to explain. He was obviously surprised and confused by my questions. He hadn't expected this procedure.

"Okay. I find the defendant guilty and assess a fine of $200 plus costs."

"Say what!" he shouted. "What you mean?"

I repeated the verdict. He looked at me, stunned.

During the next fifteen minutes we handled nine more of his cases. Each time, I fined the defendant the maximum, $200, for a total fine of $2,000 plus costs. As soon as the accumulated fines had gotten up to $2,000, I dismissed the more than ninety tickets remaining on my desk. The befuddled pimp, accompanied by his two attendants, hurried out of the courtroom, shaking his head in disbelief.

Within minutes, it seemed, the building was buzzing. Everyone knew about the case and the way I had handled it. The atmosphere in the dull traffic court building suddenly took on new life. Kangalos ran up and down the halls telling everyone who would listen how ingenious I was to fine the defendant the maximum, rather than the minimum, on each count. It seemed odd that no one had thought of this solution before.

The defendant in this case had made a disastrous error in judgment by violating the parking laws. That was a SIN, spelled in capital letters. It was permissible for drivers to run red lights, make U turns, or speed, as long as they didn't go more than fourteen or fifteen miles over the posted limit. Sure, drivers might get ticketed for such violations, but if they bothered to go to court, they knew they would get off.

Downstate, we had trials. Drivers who were found guilty, based on the evidence, were fined and acquired records that might be reflected in higher insurance premiums. Most people who received tickets simply paid them, unless there was good reason not to. In Chicago, on the other hand, simply appearing in court was an almost sure-fire way to have violations erased from the record.

Apparently, most people knew this. In 1980, only 156 thousand moving violators pleaded guilty or failed to appear and forfeited their bonds and paid fines. Most people in Chicago went to court and, as a result, were found not guilty. Again, in 1980, 665 thousand people showed up in court and 615 thousand were found not guilty. Of the remaining violators, most who were found guilty were found guilty of non-moving violations that would not appear on their licenses.

What I found most strange about the system, in the beginning, was the enormous loss of revenue. This was occurring in a city with severe financial trouble. On one hand, Chicago was having trouble paying its teachers; and on the other, it was letting thousands of traffic violators off scot-free. I was angry that drivers downstate lost their licenses as a result of moving violations, while in a metropolitan area, where mass transit systems are available, reckless drivers added to the congestion on the freeways, broke the law, and paid no penalty. It made no sense to me.

The court administrators, however, took the position that traffic court was not a fee-generating court; it was a public-minded institution in the business of rehabilitating drivers and thereby improving the city's traffic conditions. Rather than punishing drivers with official sanctions, such as fines and convictions, the philosophy of the chief judge's office was that drivers who had to spend an hour or so coming downtown and finding a place to park, and perhaps taking a day off from work, had been punished enough. They were then educated by seeing a fifteen-minute movie which was supposed to help them be better drivers in the future.

Another thing that I noticed, and thought unusual, was the number of staple marks in the drivers licenses of people who appeared in traffic court. Every time a person got a ticket, the license was stapled to the court's copy. Many of the licenses looked like they had been peppered with a shotgun. It didn't appear that motorists' driving habits were improving one bit. I had an idea there was something behind the curtain that wasn't obvious here. I was to learn more about this later.

Traffic court policy had been created by Circuit Judge Richard F. LeFevour. LeFevour had received praise from all quarters after he implemented the policy in 1971. That year, he was named presiding judge of the traffic court. His innovative approach was examined by big cities across the United States and he was recognized by the American Bar Association, from which he received an Award of Excellence. Had I been Judge LeFevour, I would have been embarrassed to accept an award for anything related to the traffic court.

Though I didn't like the situation, I decided I could live with it for six weeks a year. What the heck! The rest of the job was worthwhile. I figured I could swallow my pride for the time I was there. After all, no one from home knew what I was doing, so it wouldn't be all that demeaning.

And then, there was my curiosity about those 615 thousand motorists who, each year, were found not guilty of the traffic violations with which they had been charged. What a lot of money that represented! It could be a very big temptation to somebody.

Q: In fact, in the April 25th memorandum, you
said that you recognized that there are people
within the system who will tell people, "I fixed
the case for you" when, in fact, they hadn't. Isn't
that correct?

A: True. It is called rainmaking.

Q: Rainmaking. What is rainmaking?

A: That is a situation where the people know
ahead what a judge is doing for the day, take the
money on it, and don't do anything.

Q: Right. Just knowing the track history of a
judge, the track history of a courtroom, is that
correct?

A: Correct.

2

The Rainmaker

The United States has a crazy system of selecting judges. Most judges
are drawn from the ranks of rough and rowdy trial lawyers. Conse-
quently, we sometimes get judges whose personal and professional lives
are wild and wooly. Then, after these lawyers are elevated to the bench,
we expect them to conduct themselves with dignity and decorum.

Frankly, it was a little hard for me to play my new role as a judge—
always to be on display, so to speak. I wanted to get out of the lime-
light that comes from being a judge in a small town, so I looked
forward to the next break that Chicago offered. Though I didn't like
working in that judicial system, I did enjoy the city. It fascinated me. I
wanted to really get to know Chicago, from one end to the other—to
meet new people and see new things.

Chicago is a city of conflicts and contrasts, a city of noted saints
(Mother Cabrini) and notorious sinners (Al Capone). It is a city that
retains its own distinctive character, which Carl Sandburg described as "coarse and cutting." And it seems to have its own vitality,
particularly in the political arena. Chicago politics has a certain
flavor that I had encountered nowhere else. The politicians and the

13

press were like street fighters—and that's what the population seemed to enjoy and to want. My encounters with the city piqued my interest in the political system, the first one-party system I had ever had a chance to examine. I read everything I could about Chicago and talked to everyone I met who appeared to be "in the system." Initially, it was simply an interesting project, to discuss how and why Chicago's citizens had decided to impose a totalitarian system upon themselves. That one-party system had created and now seemed to control what was supposed to be an independent judicial system. In order to understand that judicial system, I would have to understand the city.

Chicago is a mosaic of cultures and customs, not one homogeneous community; it is made up of thousands of neighborhoods, each with its own character, language, dress, customs, and cuisine. These neighborhoods, or turfs, are drawn so as to protect those within from the outside world; they have their own leaders to represent them within the city as a whole.

To the outsider, the one-party system, referred to as The Machine, seems to be a smooth-running organization. In reality, the neighborhoods and their leadership constantly struggle for dominance, creating and breaking alliances and attempting to obtain an advantage. The Machine represents only a rather organized chaos. There is no particular loyalty to The Party, or to the organization, or to The Machine. Loyalty is to the neighborhood, the ethnic group, the family, or the gang. It certainly is not to the city as a whole. Ethnic or economic groups within the city seem to be represented by ambitious leaders who may best be described as power brokers. Power brokers have the ability to do favors for people within the neighborhood and for other power brokers and to punish those who oppose them or who fail to demonstrate sufficient loyalty. That is what Chicagoans refer to as clout.

The survival of individual power brokers depends on their ability to create a sense of safety for their followers. Within the city, people seem to feel incapable of protecting themselves or of controlling their own destinies. Black youths look to the El Rukns for survival in a hostile neighborhood. Spanish kids join the Latin Kings for physical and emotional security. The Irish cling together in the Forty-seventh

Ward. Italians cluster around the First Ward with its Cosa Nostra connections. Each group seeks to associate with a protective leader. It is reminiscent of a feudal society.

The leader is called a Chinaman—the Chicago term for power broker. There are all kinds of power brokers—politicians, wealthy businessmen, labor leaders, organized crime figures, ethnic leaders, police leaders, and street gang leaders. Leaders struggle to maintain and improve their positions within their neighborhoods and to improve the position of neighborhoods within the community as a whole. These leaders seem to have mastered the art of manipulating both followers and adversaries with a combination of financial rewards and at least the threat of physical force. Disloyal followers or competing power brokers may be "stepped on" or "buried" or financially ruined. Fear of reprisal, not loyalty to the community, is the glue that holds the city together!

True power brokers constantly play on the fears of others and show absolutely no fear themselves. In 1968, the television audience watching the Democratic National Convention was shocked when Mayor Richard Daley stood up and made obscene gestures toward the speaker's platform. However, his followers, who were accustomed to the city's rough and tumble politics, were in no way embarrassed by his antics. On the contrary, they were proud of his strength and tenacity. He was the leader because he did things that his followers would have been afraid to do.

It's hard to tell the difference sometimes between the conduct and style of a traditional power broker, or Chinaman, and a gang leader. Both have reputations for being tough, ruthless, mean, streetwise, and, of course, fearless. These are the attributes of people who can get things done in a city where most of the population feels vulnerable.

It became obvious to me that one of the important things power brokers do is handle legal cases for their constituents. This may mean taking care of building code violations for businesspeople or one of the numerous traffic cases of loyal workers. It may mean getting a light sentence for someone's brother who is faced with a serious criminal charge. Whatever the legal problem, power brokers, who serve as problem-solvers for their neighborhoods, must at least appear to have the clout to influence the outcome of a case.

Judicial decisions within the city are treated just like any other service. If a person needs his garbage picked up or his street repaired, or if the neighborhood needs lights put in or additional patrol cars, power brokers are expected to be able to help. Usually, they can—and do. Few citizens, who are isolated in the neighborhoods, would dream of going down to city hall and dealing directly with the people in charge. Instead, they go to the power brokers who serve as intermediaries. Power brokers contact the police, the mayor, or—to my surprise—the judge for help on a case.

One morning, early in my Chicago traffic court career, I got a call from someone who sounded like he was trying to imitate the Godfather. I took the telephone call in my chambers, before the first court call. Initially, I thought the call was a joke. Before I realized the caller was talking in his natural voice, I started to respond in the same gravelly whisper. Fortunately, he didn't notice. The caller, who identified himself as Alderman Vito Marzullo, said he wanted me to "take a look at" (meaning help out or take care of) a case for a close personal friend of his.

This was the first time a Chicago politician had called me directly and openly. I didn't like it. It was an insult. Usually, or so I heard, power brokers tried to go through a clerk or some other intermediary. Direct or indirect contact with a judge is a clear violation of the judicial canon of ethics. Any politician should know that rule. I assured the alderman I would take a look at the case. I was going to look all right. And I intended to penalize the defendant, whom I assumed had done something very serious. After all, if a politician took the trouble to call a judge, it must be a major problem. At any rate, I took the name and case number and had the clerk pull the file. I was surprised to see the matter had been in court once before and the defendant had been placed on supervision—a disposition that avoids a conviction and that is very lenient. Normally the defendant would be discharged on the second court date, which was that morning. Since the alderman had called, I thought perhaps the defendant had received another moving violation while on supervision, meaning that he should have his suspension revoked.

I called the secretary of state's office and asked them to run a check on the defendant's driver's license.

"There is no violation on this person's record," the clerk's voice came back.

"Are you positive?" I asked, puzzled.

"Yes, sir!"

Now my curiosity was really aroused.

When the case came up that morning, the defendant, an elderly, well-dressed, articulate businessman, stepped forward. When I questioned him at length about whether he had received any driving tickets during the time he was on supervision, he assured me that he had not. I went ahead and discharged him since he had complied with the terms of the prior supervision order.

Later, I would see this same kind of thing all the time. It's the political version of rainmaking. Alderman Marzullo's call, though meaningless to the outcome of the case, was important as far as his public relations in the neighborhood were concerned. Now in all honesty he could assure the defendant, who didn't know the ins and outs of the system, that he had called to judge to get a favor for his constituent. Thus, the constituent's loyalty to the alderman was assured.

I couldn't understand why the alderman would bother to call me when he undoubtedly knew how the case would be disposed of. I asked Joe Trunzo, a courtroom policeman with First Ward connections, why Marzullo would bother to call on an end-of-supervision case. Trunzo laughed and then explained that Marzullo was basically an honest man. Most people who understood the system would simply tell the constituent they would call, but they wouldn't bother to do it. Marzullo, on the other hand, was a man of his word. He would actually make the call. He had one rule—he would never lie to a constituent. Apparently, he would rather perform a meaningless act than fail to keep his word. This was called honest rainmaking.

Some time after this incident, I read Mike Royko's book, *Boss*. I was amused to see that, according to Royko, Vito Marzullo had a long history of involvement with the judiciary. Years ago, as a display of his prestige, Marzullo had a full circuit judge accompany him everywhere he went—just to open doors. No wonder he didn't hesitate to call a judge directly and ask for a favor.

Eventually, I was to learn that do-me-a-favor calls were commonplace. Most of the time, however, the power brokers did not deal with sitting judges directly—especially downstate judges. The normal procedure was to deal with the people in the front office—the bailiwick of Richard LeFevour.

Initially, I thought traffic court was chaotic. Later, I learned it was really quite orderly—even more orderly than an ant colony, of which it often reminded me. From behind the scenes, one of the city's most powerful Chinamen controlled every movement, every decision, made in the traffic court building. Because each group that works within the system produces its own power brokers, it is not surprising that the judiciary, which is an offshoot of the political system, would do the same.

To be a judge—a good, fair judge—takes a lot of courage. It is extremely hard to look a man right in the eye and tell him that he did wrong and that you are going to punish him for it. This is made substantially easier in Chicago, however, where few judges do that.

For the most part, the judges I met in trial court had been placed there by politicians or the power brokers, either legally or otherwise. Generally, they were people whom the power brokers knew they could control. And I found many—or even most—to be weak, ineffectual, timid men who were fearful of making anyone angry. They were always concerned that the defendant would have some power broker in his hip pocket—someone who would get revenge on the judge who decided a case on its merits. Political realities, they believed, would never allow such a foolish decision. The timid souls on the bench seemed to "do everybody a favor," and thus they avoided imposing any severe sanctions on anyone. It is a chummy way to handle things, but justice gets lost in the shuffle.

Besides power brokers, Chicago judges are concerned primarily about the assignment judge—the person who supervises a group of judges assigned to his particular area. The assignment judge has the power to figuratively bury any of his subordinates in a bad assignment. The biggest power broker in the judiciary was Judge Richard LeFevour, who was variously called The Chief or The King. Judge LeFevour was assignment judge for the traffic court, and later for the First Municipal District. His sources of power and influence allowed him to make "his" judges and other underlings believe he could literally, as well as figuratively, bury them.

From the first time I met him, I felt uncomfortable with Judge LeFevour. He had a cold arrogance, which I detested, and was frequently angry. My first exposure to LeFevour's influence, a rather innocuous contact with policeman Ira Blackwood, occurred during my first fill-in assignment in Chicago. I had been introduced to Ira by another downstate judge and had spent an evening on the town, getting better acquainted. Ira was a patrolman assigned to supervise police officers who appeared in court, and it was soon obvious that he knew his way around. One morning I met Ira in my chambers. He asked me in an offhand manner whether I gave the traffic safety movie to "twelve over"—meaning those who had been arrested for driving twelve miles an hour over the speed limit.

I shrugged. "No. I just discharge them en masse." Ira laughed.

He told me that the front office had called and asked him to take care of a speeder, an IRS agent who had been caught doing twelve miles over the speed limit. Ira explained casually that it was a personal favor for Judge LeFevour. I had an idea Ira was asking for the favor because The King wanted him to size me up—to gauge my reaction to such a request. At the time, I hadn't met LeFevour, but I had heard plenty about him. And even though I was beginning to be wise to requests for favors, I was still surprised by Ira's request on behalf of Judge LeFevour.

I couldn't imagine I was being asked by the assignment judge to fix a case. But I didn't feel secure enough yet in my own position to lodge any complaints against him. I told Ira the IRS agent would get the same treatment as everyone else—which satisfied the policeman.

That morning I took the bench and started my talk about the difference between justice (the downstate system), and mercy (the Chicago counterpart). I was interrupted by Gino Superchi,* one of Judge LeFevour's assistants.

"You are being transferred immediately to Courtroom 16," Superchi whispered.

"Why, for God's sake?" I asked.

*Pseudonym.

"Chiefs orders. Let's go."

I apologized to the audience and was ushered at once to the appropriate courtroom. I was perplexed until I saw Ira later in the day. He said I had been transferred because the IRS agent was too important to take a chance on. LeFevour had put one of his regulars in my chair to guarantee the outcome.

After that, I learned fast about the Chicago system of justice.

In the quick shuffle, I had been transferred to Room 16, which handles taxi violations. I was not familiar with the ordinances involved or the procedures which were followed in that room, and no one had time to fill me in. I simply took the bench, assuming it was the same kind of courtroom I had just left—the minor movers, where everyone got a break.

Again, I gave my talk and began to handle the first case. Corporation counsel who was supposed to prosecute the cases that morning was an ancient war horse named Morrie, who slept through most of the call. My clerk was Harold Conn. He would be the first defendant tried and convicted in the Greylord cases. At the time, as far as I knew, Conn was an honest and efficient man. He handled his job well, called the cases, and we went about our business without a prosecutor. Our bailiff was named Sam Cline. He was eighty years old, and a stroke had left one arm withered with paralysis. Sam had been a bodyguard for Al Capone.

Conn started calling the jitney cases, which turned out to be charges against unlicensed taxicab drivers. Not knowing any better, and without any help from the sleeping Morrie, I simply lectured the taxicab drivers and then sent them to the safety movie or discharged them outright.

Suddenly, the courtroom was full of people urging me to take a break. Bert Pillar* from the traffic division of corporation counsel's office; Superchi, LeFevour's assistant; somebody I didn't know from the clerk's office; and Ira Blackwood all wanted to talk to me at the same time. I called a recess.

Ira handed me a copy of the various ordinances involved and ex-

*Pseudonym.

plained that the city actually wanted to have taxicab cases determined on their merits. I couldn't believe it. I remember thinking it was odd that Blackwood, a patrolman, and not Pillar, from corporation counsel, would bring the ordinances to my attention. Who was running what in this madhouse?

The thing that baffled me was that this time they actually wanted to make unlicensed drivers pay fines. It turned out that the licensed drivers were all connected with city hall, and the mayor's office had already gotten wind of the fact that I was not protecting their rights. I assured everyone if they wanted me actually to decide the cases on the merits, I was all for that. We would just go right in and go to work. I was happy to have something real to do for a change. Unfortunately, as soon as I finished the next call, I was hustled back to my original courtroom. By this time, the case of the IRS agent had been dismissed.

It was probably two years before I got back into Room 16. Little had changed except that perhaps Morrie snored a little louder. Sam Cline had been replaced. He had suffered another stroke and was confined to bed. Conn was still there, awake and efficient. He called the cases and I disposed of them.

That morning I had been moved to Room 16, I met Judge John J. Devine, the judge who had been sent in by LeFevour to make sure the case against the IRS agent was dismissed. My dislike of Devine was nearly automatic. He had a personal bailiff, which usually meant bagman. In Devine's case it meant slave. The bailiff, an older fellow named Rocky, talked like Rocky Balboa. Every day, after our first meeting, Rocky would be in the hall, smiling and politely bowing when I walked in.

"How ya doin', Judge? How's the family?"

The same question every day, and always pleasant, always loyal—to the judges and to the system. As far as I know, Rocky was a gracious gentleman.

Judge Devine appeared to get a vicious pleasure from criticizing Rocky in front of other people. He used Rocky as his personal valet, sending him to run errands, buy groceries and liquor, and clean his car. This had to be done quite often because of the judge's accidents on his way home from the bars. Devine had a little mustache that made him look like a 1930s villain, and he fit the part perfectly.

Eventually he made the mistake of crossing Judge LeFevour, and he was buried in a branch court. Out of sight, out of mind, out of bribe money. Devine would be one of the first judges indicted in Operation Greylord, four years after our first meeting.

Most of LeFevour's regular judges—the ones who worked the major rooms where serious traffic cases were heard—appeared to be surly individuals who, it was rumored, drank too much, even on the job. There were five of them, initially, who worked four major rooms. I'd heard Ira Blackwood say about each of them—at one time or another—"Boy, is he an obnoxious bastard!" Of course, the way Ira said that, I never knew if it was a compliment or a derogatory remark. My reaction to most of these characters was similar to my reaction to Judge Devine. I found them to be offensive bores.

On the other hand, while Judge LeFevour made me uncomfortable, he also fascinated me. Everywhere I turned, he seemed to have developed alliances with powerful supporters. Either through his family relationships or his friends, he seemed to control everything and everyone in one hell of a big area. No doubt about it, the title, King, fit him well. It was no surprise he was the judge who swore in Rich Daley as Chicago's state's attorney in 1980! (This association probably shouldn't be held against Daley. As far as I know, Richard Daley is an honest man.)

The point is that LeFevour worked at attempting to be "close friends" with the various factions of the Democratic party: Dunne, Kelly, Byrne, and Vrdolyak were all people that he claimed as allies. He also insisted that he was a close personal friend of United States congressman Dan Rostenkowski. Later, when Judge LeFevour moved over to the Daley Center to take charge of the First Municipal District, he employed Rostenkowski's sister as a receptionist.

I have no reason to think that any of these political personages were in any way involved with Judge LeFevour's illegal activities. It served LeFevour's purposes to drop the names of the rich and famous and be photographed with them at every opportunity. Obviously, Judge LeFevour did have friends in the right places. However, I suspect that many of his "close friends" were no more than acquaintances.

As evidence of his connections and power, LeFevour was appointed to the coveted position of marshal of the St. Patrick's Day parade in 1979. His office walls were covered with numerous awards from both the legal and the lay community, in recognition of the way he ran the traffic court building. LeFevour was strong to the point of being ruthless, but he could also be witty and charming. Surprisingly, these contrasts in personality worked well for him. Most people, including myself, were a little afraid of him. Many courthouse people told stories of how he had crushed various individuals who got in his way. I saw the man only on rare occasions, so some of my impressions about him are vague. He was gaunt looking—perhaps six feet tall— with deep set, rather sullen, eyes. He had an expressive face that quickly showed his moods. He could easily have been mistaken for the classic image of a funeral director.

Judge LeFevour was the son of a police captain. In some ways, he seemed to prefer associating with policemen, deputies, and clerks rather than with judges. Perhaps he reflected some parental attitudes because he seemed to despise most of the judges who worked under him. Of course, they were weak and ineffectual, but they were the kind of judges he wanted. They were easier to manipulate and control.

I went into LeFevour's office one Friday morning to get permission to leave at noon. Although he allowed "downstate" or "country" judges off early to go home at the end of the week, we always had to ask him for the privilege. We were expected to go to his office and make small talk for awhile before we brought up the subject of leaving early. Judge LeFevour was what some people called a basic fellow. He was much more interested in locker room discussions than in court business. The judge's primary interest seemed to be some female clerk's or deputy's physical attributes. His conversations certainly didn't build respect for, or bring honor to, the judiciary.

On one particular Friday, as I was ready to request permission to return home early, a large black woman stormed into the King's inner office, her face tight with anger. She screamed at LeFevour, "There's a clerk in Room 12 who is prejudiced and a bigot!"

LeFevour leaned forward in his chair and stared at the woman. He looked cold as a corpse. In a voice loud enough for everyone in the outer office to hear, he snarled, "And so am I. Now get the hell out of my office."

The woman stood in stunned silence for a minute, then turned and left, meek as a child sent to her room. The King smiled and winked at me as she left. He loved to show off his power.

Q: Mr. Lockwood, did this conduct that you observed focus on any particular individual, and did you address the Justice Department in terms of a particular person?

A: The concern I had was that the person who was running the traffic court building at the time seemed to be supervising and engaging in all kinds of criminal or unlawful conduct, besides unethical conduct, and that was the focus of my attention, really.

Q: Who was that individual?

A: That was Judge LeFevour.

Q: His first name is what?

A: Richard.

3

The Open Drawer Policy

I have always been a people-watcher, and the variety of subjects available to watch in downtown Chicago is tremendous—everything from rags to riches.

I'm from a small town, so in Chicago I noticed how people walking to work pass each other, apparently without seeing one another. Not only was there no smile or nod, there was simply no expression of any kind. People didn't react even when they were bumped or when a particularly shrill noise sounded. I wondered if they had lost all sense of perception. Perhaps their nerve endings had been frozen or blown away with the wind. I don't know.

But it was only on the street that people seemed to be so dehumanized. Once in the shelter of the traffic court building on LaSalle Street, I noticed a miraculous change. Everyone appeared friendly and animated. I looked forward to the cheery greetings when I walked into the building. Initially, I didn't understand the motivation behind the friendliness.

As I entered the building there would be a chorus of:

"Good morning, Judge."

"How's the family?"

"Got a big call today?"

There would be smiles, handshakes, arm squeezes, and pats on the back.

"You're looking great, Judge!"

My first impression was that many of the court personnel were substantially older than might normally be expected. Many people retire when they're sixty-five years of age. But Chicago is "the city that works." Every loyal Democrat has a job . . . forever it seems. As a result, people in the courtrooms were working into their eighties. The jobs weren't demanding, and because many of these people performed adequately, it seemed like a great idea. I was sure they were happier than they would have been sitting at home in a lonely apartment.

My later, more studied, impression about the people in the traffic court building was that they were the most listless group I had ever seen — totally bored with their jobs. Even the new people coming into the system seemed to be there just to put in their time. No one seemed to feel it was important to do a good job — or even to know what that job was. No one seemed to care about anything other than getting through the day with as little effort as possible and then rushing out of the building. The atmosphere in the building was dismal. People seemed tired and discouraged, and they complained frequently about illnesses or personal problems or expressed other gripes of one kind or another.

Many employees had no idea what went on within the system, and they didn't seem to care about the functions of other departments. Their lives were tedious, and they had few outside interests. They were like moles that never left their burrows. Sadly, they seemed resigned to it.

By contrast, my life seemed extremely interesting to them. They wanted me to tell stories about people and cases in southern Illinois, about the farm, and about my race horses. I would hear my stories repeated and exaggerated later. It was strange how much attention I got just by breaking the deadly monotony in the building.

I liked these people, and at the same time I felt sorry for them. Life in the big city can be extremely dull without enough money to enjoy the entertainment. And people who work in public service usually don't earn enough to do more than make ends meet.

I was particularly amazed at the lack of interest expressed by new attorneys coming into the corporation counsel's office. Downstate, state's attorney's offices recruit new attorneys who learn to be trial lawyers by prosecuting traffic and misdemeanor cases. They are usually enthusiastic about their jobs, and they are eager to learn how to operate in the courtroom. In Chicago, however, the new recruits to the corporation counsel's office were frequently older people, people in their sixties, who were burned out before they ever started. Even the younger attorneys appeared to be bored when they arrived at work. Their only goal seemed to be earning a paycheck while they established a private practice on the side. It appeared that no one had any intention of actually becoming a trial lawyer or learning how to prosecute a case.

In the beginning I was amazed that the prosecutors seemed to be nonentities within the Chicago court system. Downstate, the judge, sitting as a neutral umpire, frequently has to restrain the over-zealous prosecutor who tries to exceed his official powers. By contrast, in Chicago the prosecutors actually slowed down the whole system.

After a few weeks in traffic court, I asked the head of corporation counsel not to bother sending a prosecutor. The way he handled this request was unique. The director would assign someone to me who had more important things to to . . . and he just wouldn't show up.

No one seemed upset. No one cared.

I was naive about the system at first. But the more I learned about traffic court and how it worked, the more it fascinated me. The general confusion throughout the building had led me to think the system was unstructured. Gradually, however, I began to discover it was a well-ordered society. Every one had a place and rank within the structure—the structure behind the scenes that most employees thought it best not to see. It was a closed society, and only people with sponsors who would vouch for them could ever get in. The process depended on allegiances. Someone helped you, so you owed them. You paid them back. Then, maybe they owed you. It was a tightly organized political system—as tightly organized as any feudal system.

During my second tour in 1979, after the first few weeks in traffic court, I became aware that most people seemed to be doing favors for someone else. This puzzled me considerably because I couldn't see that they got anything in return. I assumed they were used to doing political favors, and this was a way of paying their dues. I did not like the idea of politicians invading the courthouse, but I failed to recognize that I was living in a den of thieves. It was all done so smoothly, so nonchalantly, that I was caught off guard.

My awareness of the corruption within the system really began one morning when an attorney berated my clerk for losing a file. I couldn't understand why the attorney was so angry. Given the number of files in that building, it seemed to me it would be easy to lose one. After work, I joined several of the clerks for drinks. Curiosity and a bit of suspicion about the event led to a discussion with a clerk who had been present that morning. He explained that the attorney had refused to tip the clerk in question when calling the case, so the clerk had simply lost the file. I couldn't believe what I was hearing—or how casually it was being told to me.

I bought more drinks and began to broaden the discussion about tips. I was told that the cost varied, depending on the attorney's business. A clerk might charge a new lawyer five dollars a case to get him in and out quickly. The older lawyers paid a specified amount each week, depending on their business.

I tried to act as if I were getting drunk, and I asked more questions, trying not to seem eager. The clerks were getting a lot drunker than I was, thank God. They tried to impress me with how much the big boys in the building made. It began to seem as if almost all support personnel could be taking money. The clerks, the deputies, the police —they all made money doing favors for defendants and their attorneys.

I went to bed that night wondering if what I'd been told was the truth. The longer I lay awake, the sharper the picture of corruption became. It all made sense. Things tied together. A lot of people had too much money, without salaries to justify it. Too many things added up for it not to be true.

A more frightening thought hit me. If I believed what was said that night, then I had to decide what to do about it. A cloud of depression settled over me. I was numb.

The next day the offending clerk made it worse. During a break, he used the telephone in my chambers to call his stockbroker. He wanted to know where he could deposit $100,000 for the greatest return. A court clerk with $100,000 to toss around? I couldn't believe it. Two days later, before court, I heard the same clerk tell an attorney, "We have an open drawer policy here." The phrase was not new to me. The evening I drank with the clerks, they had explained it was customary for a clerk simply to open a desk drawer and let the attorney drop the tips in.

My God! It was all handled so casually. I shook my head.

I thought about whether to report the clerk to the chief presiding judge, Richard LeFevour. I didn't feel comfortable doing that, however, because I had no proof against the man. I didn't even know the name of the attorney with whom he had originally crossed swords.

But that was LeFevour's problem. Not mine.

Before I did anything more, however, I got to know LeFevour's administrative assistant, Gino Superchi. He was a young man, perhaps thirty years old, who looked and dressed like a movie star. It was January, and Superchi had an Acapulco tan. He told me that he had, in fact, just returned from Mexico. He had bet twenty-five thousand dollars on the Super Bowl and won. He claimed he had blown his winnings on a vacation with two Honey Bears—cheerleaders for the Chicago Bears.

The salary for an administrative assistant is probably twenty thousand dollars a year. Suddenly, I was more suspicious of Superchi than I was of the clerk. I did some checking and discovered Superchi was connected with the First Ward. It doesn't take very long in Chicago to figure out what that means. First Ward means Mafia. In years past, the Forty-seventh Ward got all the good positions. The recipients were always Irish. More recently, with the political changes in the city, the Italian wards now carried the most clout.

Drinking cronies freely answered my questions about the administrative assistant and his First Ward connection. Superchi was recognized as the Chief's bagman. At the time, I didn't know that a bagman is a money messenger. I also discovered that Superchi and the head of the corporation counsel's office, Bert Pillar,* had a lot in

*Pseudonym.

common. Not only were they both from the First Ward, they also traveled in the same social group and had the same tailor.

During January and February, I began to spend time with several people from the corporation counsel's office, the pool of attorneys who were prosecutors for traffic court. I was curious about their boss Bert Pillar, about LeFevour's administrative assistant, and about what else might be going on in the building. In my effort to satisfy that curiosity, I cultivated Tommie Kangalos, an attorney from the corporation counsel's office. I had been looking for a source of information, and when I met Tommie, I knew I had found that source. He had a certain air about him, as if seeking to impress everyone with how much he knew. I sensed he was the kind who would talk.

At the last moment, I held back. This was a hell of a big step I was about to take. My career could be at stake if I made the wrong move. It would be easier just to put blinders on. I wanted to know the rest of the story, but another part of me was saying, "See nothing, hear nothing, do nothing. It's none of your damned business." Finally I couldn't stand not knowing. I plunged ahead.

I began to socialize with Tommie frequently. Most of the time, if we were in a restaurant, he drank martinis. That was good—gin loosened his tongue. We would exchange stories as I led him gently on. I'd tell him about the "good ole boys" from the South, and he would tell me about all the "sharp cookies" from city hall and the scams they were involved with. He was bent on impressing me with his power, his money, and his influence. I encouraged him.

Tommie repeatedly told me he didn't know how to practice law, but he intended to be the biggest bagman in the city before he was done. He always bought the drinks, dinner, or whatever. And while he drank, he talked. His brashness fascinated me. I'd never known anyone who would tell a judge about the illegal conduct in which he was involved. But Tommie loved to talk.

I should have told him I didn't approve, I suppose; instead, I continued to lead him on, acting as if I believed he was a wheel. I told him I needed to learn what was going on, just to protect my own skin. He explained that I was just like he was initially. As soon as he got into the traffic court building, he knew something wasn't right, and he decided to learn the score so he could get in on the big money. We talked about several scams, some of which had been pulled on me—and I hadn't known it! Tommie got a big laugh out of that.

A frequent scam used by the people in corporation counsel's office was simply to dismiss cases for defendants. The prosecuting attorney would receive the bond money after having the judge sign a bond assignment form. Then he could simply pocket the money.

Proving this had happened would be another matter.

Tommie was a talking encyclopedia. I sought him out at every opportunity and I encouraged him in every way to share his great wealth of knowledge about city hall. It seemed that everyone in the system was in a position to receive payments from potential defendants who were concerned about the disposition of their cases. Those within the system knew what the disposition would be with any particular judge. They would look at the defendant's ticket, and for the right price, usually thirty-five to fifty dollars, they could guarantee the defendant would receive whatever sentence that the judge usually handed out.

For instance, clerks assigned to courtrooms in which the less serious cases were handled knew the usual sentence was to watch a fifteen-minute movie on traffic safety. The clerk would simply tell the defendant, "I'll talk to the judge and I'll get the movie for you for thirty-five dollars." The unsuspecting defendant would think he was getting a real break. He was glad to pay the money. The clerk probably would not even have to say anything to the judge. If he did, he would simply say, "Judge, would you mind taking a look at this case. If you can do anything, I'd appreciate it; this man is a friend of mine." The unsuspecting judges in the minor courtrooms had no idea that this innocuous request would turn into a thirty-five dollar bribe, referred to as a fee.

There are always deputies at the entrances to the traffic court building. They are there to help citizens find their way around. The traffic court building is relatively large, with seventeen courtrooms in all. Two floors are occupied by traffic courtrooms. Thus, assistance in finding the right room is sometimes necessary.

Other forms of assistance are also available.

Of all the hustlers in the building, one stands out as the most professional and businesslike: a deputy sheriff who stood near the front entrance. He was assigned to this place every morning to give directions to newcomers to the building. It takes a lot of time—and influence—to get a good position like this within the system. In addition to giving directions, the deputy would engage in a little rainmaking—taking credit for an outcome over which he really had no control. The hustler who knows how the system works, and what a particular judge will do, can convince a violator to pay him for getting an outcome on a ticket that is acceptable to the violator—an outcome that he would have gotten anyway.

As I indicated earlier, politicians did it for power. People in the traffic court building did it for money.

At any rate, the deputy at the front door had the first opportunity to "assist" traffic offenders with their problems. He would look at a ticket, feign concern for the plight of the offender, and assure him that he could help him out of the situation. The deputy would explain that, unfortunately, this case would be heard by a very tough judge. However, because this judge just happened to be a close personal friend of the deputy, the deputy could help the offender—for a price. For thirty-five dollars, the deputy would agree to speak to the judge, to be sure that the defendant was sent to the movie. This same scam was being worked up and down the hall by deputies, clerks, bailiffs, and anyone else who happened to be in the know.

The unique aspect of the front door deputy's operation was that he didn't bother to go to the courtroom to collect his fee before the offender left the building. He didn't have time to leave his post! The deputy just took down the offender's name and address and gave him an envelope to mail in his fee. If the fee wasn't received on time, the deputy would send the defendant a reminder postcard. It was quite a business!

I learned from Tommie about another scam prevalent in the building. Several people from corporation counsel's office were involved with the multiple parking section, an area where people who had more than ten parking tickets were handled. Normal procedure was that a case would be settled for 50 percent of the amount owed, at twenty dollars per ticket.

But instead of the money for these tickets going to the city, it was diverted to the corporation counsel who handled the case and to the judge who would put the offender on court supervision. The defendant was unaware he had been placed on court supervision for a period of time, and after court supervision ended, he would not have a record. In these cases, the judge did not impose a fine. The payment of 50 percent of the minimum fine was required as a cash bond and was collected by the warrant officer. The cash was then split among the warrant officer, the attorney, and the judge. The defendant would never know that his money was not, in fact, deposited with the city. All the defendant was concerned about was that the warrant for his arrest was quashed and the tickets taken care of.

According to Tommie, the judge who handled the parking violations received hundreds of thousands of dollars in revenues from this enterprise. That judge was the presiding judge of traffic court — Richard LeFevour.

Parking was not LeFevour's only illegal enterprise. There are four major traffic violation courtrooms where cases that involve potential jail sentences are handled. The charges include driving under the influence of alcohol, driving while a license is suspended or revoked, or fleeing or attempting to elude a police officer. These cases are handled by the state's attorney's office rather than by corporation counsel's office. Tommie claimed that he could fix any case in those rooms by going to one of the judges directly. Apparently the people in the state's attorney's office were not in on the deal.

Usually, Tommie said, in a difficult case he would take care of the officer for maybe one hundred dollars and the judge for two hundred dollars. Again, according to Tommie, the judges assigned to the major rooms had to pay LeFevour a certain amount of rent each week to keep their assignments to the lucrative courtrooms. Whatever a judge received from the attorneys was his own business.

Tommie told me, and I heard it from several other sources later, that LeFevour was the first judge to make a million dollars out of the traffic court assignment. This accomplishment had made him a sort of folk-hero to people in the system.

At the time of these discussions, I was running around not only with Tommie, but also with another corporation counsel assistant, a young man named Carl Harper,* just out of law school at Southern Illinois University. We spent time at Rush Street, enjoying the city's night life. From what Tommie had told me, I knew that Carl was a bagman for Bert Pillar, head of the corporation counsel's office. I expressed my concern to Carl for his safety. He seemed to be a nice kid, very bright and personable, with the potential to become a top-rate lawyer.

He and Tommie both assured me that there were no risks involved. They were convinced that the state's attorney's office would not touch them—or for that matter was even aware of their activities—and that no federal violations were involved. They seemed to feel they were immune from prosecution.

I was depressed by the knowledge that Tommie and Carl were probably right. At the same time, however, I was determined to seek out the extent of judicial corruption in traffic court. I was not considered one of the boys, and I was getting all the information on the court's illegal operations that I could want.

In the spring of 1980, the city was in the thick of the primary election. In addition to spending evenings at Rush Street with people from the traffic court building, I went to some political fundraisers. This conduct would not be permitted downstate. Judges, unless they are running for office, do not participate in any political activities. In Chicago, my observation was that all the judges participated heavily. They not only attended the fundraisers, they contributed to campaigns. One evening, Carl Harper asked me to go to a fundraiser at BBC, a Rush Street disco. The event was being held for a local candidate running in the Democratic primary. Carl had free tickets. He told me that his boss, Bert Pillar, was sponsoring the event, and he was giving away twenty-five-dollar tickets. I was not a particular fan of the candidate, but I was curious about the fundraiser.

BBC is a large establishment, occupying the second and third stories of a building just off Rush Street, at the north end of the entertainment section. On the evening of the fundraiser, it was packed. Curiously, the people attending the function were not old political contributors or party members. They were young, attractive Rush Street people. And everyone I met had free tickets. This didn't make sense—not for a fundraising event.

When Tommie Kangalos arrived, he cleared up the mystery. He pointed out three tables, off to the side. At one table were Mike Jackson* and some of his associates. Jackson, an attorney and city commissioner, served as political spokesman for the First Ward. At another table were three old men that Tommie referred to as Mustache Petes—they seemed out of place. At the third table sat several muscular men—bodyguards—who looked as if they were out of a Grade B movie.

Tommie explained that this was a First Ward party—"A very important party," he stressed. To show their support for the candidate, the "big moguls of First Ward" (Tommie's words) had purchased all the tickets and given them away to friends. The people from corporation counsels' office and, sure enough, LeFevour's administrative assistants, were sitting at Jackson's table—a place usually reserved for honored guests.

Oddly, Tommie seemed as uncomfortable as I was. He told me not to sign the guest register at the entrance. I hadn't signed it because I did not want to be associated with the fundraiser, but I told Tommie that I had signed his name. He looked a little sick until I smiled.

Tommie might have been afraid of the FIRST WARD. But I felt a twinge of fear, too—fear that I was getting to know too much about the corruption that was poisoning the Chicago courts.

I came home in the spring of 1980 feeling ashamed and guilty because I had remained silent. I had observed all this corruption, but I had done nothing about it.

Why didn't I report it?

I was afraid of the principals—of LeFevour, of his assistant, and, now, of the Mafia. I was also afraid of being caught doing something wrong in that system. I became paranoid about everyone I met who was connected with the court system, afraid something might be done without my knowledge and that I or my family would be embarrassed—or worse. I was afraid that I would be framed for doing

*Pseudonym.

something illegal—arrested and charged with some crime. My fear made me ashamed of myself.

But three hundred fifty miles from Chicago—at home in southern Illinois—I began to get more courageous. Fear turned slowly to anger and then to resentment. At first I thought I would simply expose the system and then quit. But, damn it, how would I report it?

I wanted to contact Mike Royko at the Chicago *Sun-Times*. In a Rush Street bar, I had met a woman who worked at the *Sun-Times*, so I called her to see if she could arrange an introduction. I talked with her boss, who was not interested because judicial corruption was not newsworthy and probably libelous. I did not pursue it further.

It hadn't been a good idea to contact the media in the first place. I probably would have exposed my identity had the action gone further. Then I would have had to quit my job without accomplishing anything at all. And the results might might have been even worse. I guess I wanted it both ways—I wanted to keep my job as a circuit judge, but at the same time I wanted to do something about the corruption.

I considered trying to have the problem handled within the judicial system and wrote a long letter to the supreme court administrator, Judge Roy Gulley, a southern Illinois native. I believed him to be an honest man, and thought he might be in a position to do something.

All that I reasonably hoped for at the moment was that downstate judges would no longer have to be assigned to the court mess in Chicago. I certainly didn't expect to change anything within the Chicago system. The problems were too deeply entrenched.

In the letter to Judge Gulley I outlined what was going on in Chicago and suggested that we downstate judges be relieved of our assignments there. I worried over the letter for several days and finally showed it to Robert Chase, chief judge of the First Judicial Circuit.

When Judge Chase asked me what I expected Gulley to do about the situation, I had to admit that he couldn't really do anything. I had no proof, no evidence—just a lot of personal observation. Sending the letter might be risky as far as my future was concerned. Without hard evidence, I was only spreading rumors. It was a dead end. I didn't send the letter.

For several months I remained in a state of turmoil, afraid to do anything. Frankly, I was fearful of losing my job. I would be stepping on too many big toes.

There are many different kinds of fear. Some are positive—the kind that makes the adrenelin flow in the face of danger. I was involved in football and wrestling in high school and was carried along on an emotional high produced by fear—fear of losing. I had the same feeling when I was trying cases. But this fear was something different. It was cowardly—negative and depressing. I could easily rationalize not doing anything about the problems in Chicago. After all, they weren't my problems, and I couldn't solve them. There was no possibility that I could ever stop corruption in the Chicago judiciary system. I was a fool even to think about it.

Still, knowing what was going on and not doing something about it was, in my mind, tantamount to participating in the corruption. My grandfather's values—firmly entrenched—convinced me that to do nothing was unacceptable.

I was ashamed of myself, and I was no longer proud of the position I held. In the summer of 1980, I decided the job was not worth keeping. I hadn't agreed to become a judge in a corrupt system—even on a part-time basis. If that was part of the job, they could have it.

Once I made that decision, I felt a lot better. I still had no idea what I was going to do about my next assignment to the city. I had almost decided to refuse it and take the consequences.

Then, fate entered the picture. I was given the opportunity to accept a fill-in assignment in Waukegan, Illinois. I jumped at the chance. Temporarily, I was able—with clear conscience, I thought—to avoid the issue.

But sometime in the fall of 1980, I realized I was still playing the coward. I decided that after the presidential election I would contact the Justice Department in Washington, D.C. This absolutely would be my last attempt to do something about the Chicago mess.

Q: I direct your attention to the latter part of
1980 and the early part of 1981. Did you at that
time have occasion to contact the Department of
Justice in Washington?

A: Yes, I did.

Q: In what regard did you contact the Justice
Department?

A: I was concerned about indications and
evidence of judicial corruption initially in the
traffic court building.

Q: Was it in that regard that you contacted the
Justice Department?

A: Yes, I did.

4

The Invisible Man Becomes "Winston"

The presidential election was over. Ronald Reagan had swept into
office on a landslide.

I remembered the promise I had made to myself earlier. It was time
to take official action about the Chicago mess, and to hell with the
consequences.

I've always operated on the premise that, when you don't know
whom to trust, start at the top. I called the Justice Department in
Washington. They agreed to send someone to meet me in Chicago.

The federal building on Adams Street is actually a complex of three
structures—twin matte black steel monoliths that rise twenty-seven
stories, almost menacingly, against the Chicago skyline, and a
matching long, low building that houses the downtown post office.
The only relief to the Federal Plaza's somber atmosphere is one of the
city's famed outdoor sculptures: a fire engine red double slash of
curving steel. As a metaphor for the city, the sculpture is right on
target—powerful, without much taste or subtlety.

On a late afternoon in February 1981, as I approached the easternmost structure, the Everett M. Dirksen Building, I tugged my parka hood closer about my face. Almost without thinking, I tried to hide my moustache under my hand. With a suit, a trench coat would have been more suitable; it also would have been darkly appropriate to my appointment. But I had opted for the parka. I could conceal more of myself in it. I felt particularly foolish—almost like a criminal myself—huddling in my coat as I boarded the elevator; but my fear of being recognized outweighed my concern over social embarrassment. Traffic court was all of seven wintry, windswept blocks north, but I wanted no one to know I had business in the federal building.

By now I was suspicious of everyone. I could see a ghost behind every door.

Room 1576 was right where it was supposed to be. I entered, trying to get the parka off before the secretary noticed me. She tactfully steered me to an empty waiting room, apparently to spare me contact with any chance visitors. I sat there for a few minutes, trying to calm myself. Then I noticed the window blinds were open. The occupants of adjoining buildings had a clear view into the room. Hurriedly I twisted the blinds shut, then quickly sat back down. I was panting— from fear and nervousness, I'm sure.

Again, I posed to myself the difficult question, "What in the hell am I getting myself into?"

But the time had come to tell what I knew. I had been afraid to approach the federal authorities while Jimmy Carter and Ronald Reagan were slugging it out. I didn't want anyone deciding to make judicial corruption a national issue. But now—here I was. There was no backing down this time.

I confess that, though I have been a dutiful Democrat most of my life, I was somewhat relieved to be contacting a Republican administration. I hoped Chicago's Democratic machine wouldn't be able to reach deep into Reagan's organization, although Tommie Kangalos had told me enough to make me wonder.

My previous experience with a Republican administration hadn't been exactly faith-inspiring. In 1968, while I worked as a student assistant for a U.S. attorney in Nashville, I had a close-up view of Nixon's attorney general, John Mitchell, quashing indictments in anti-trust cases. But despite my reservations, I was determined to contact the government, tell my story, and point the investigators in the right direction. Then I'd resign from the judiciary and forget the whole sordid mess. This was to be my parting shot at a job that had caused me so much anxiety and frustration.

I thought back over the events that had brought me to this room. After I made my decision, I hardly wanted to trust my fate to a U.S. Department of Justice switchboard operator. I asked a Marion attorney, who would be attending Reagan's inaugural ball, to get me the name of someone reliable in the Justice Department's Public Integrity section. As far as my Republican attorney friend knew, that request concerned corruption in southern Illinois. He brought me the telephone number of Gerald McDowell, a division head on Attorney General William French Smith's staff. My friend assured me that McDowell was reputed to be "very straight" and an effective attorney.

I called McDowell, but the answering secretary refused to put the call through or even to have McDowell return my call unless I told her the nature of my business. So much for influential friends. The secretary hadn't appreciated my telling her I was not going to discuss my business with her, but she finally put me through to Sam Forstein, an attorney who worked for McDowell.

Disclosing sensitive information over the telephone to a complete stranger was not what I had in mind. But, after questioning Forstein about his background and credentials, I decided to trust him. His confession that he knew little about Chicago or its politics cinched it.

I told Forstein I was a state associate judge from southern Illinois, who frequently was assigned to Chicago. As a result, I had information about misconduct within Chicago's judicial system. I wanted to disclose that information to the Department of Justice. I explained that I was hesitant to disclose the information to the U.S. attorney in Chicago for fear it might be passed on to powerful and potentially dangerous city authorities; but I didn't know whether the federal government had jurisdiction over the situations that I wanted to discuss.

Forstein agreed to let me talk to someone who was not associated with the U.S. attorney's office in Chicago. I suggested he contact the FBI office in Carbondale—the one nearest my home—to check me out before he proceeded. I had shared an office building with the FBI when I was a practicing attorney there, and most of the agents would know me. Forstein never checked me out as far as I know; but he did call me back at the Williamson County courthouse, learning at least that a judge named Brocton Lockwood worked there. After that he arranged for me to meet with him and Larry Beck, another Justice Department attorney, during my next stint in Chicago, in the first part of February 1981. I forwarded a summary of what I had to disclose, and then I tried to keep calm and prayed that I was moving in the right direction.

As the time for our meeting approached, I brooded on the potential for leaks. I created all kinds of worrisome scenarios that kept me awake at night. For instance, an unwitting Justice Department attorney would pass along what I said to the U.S. attorney in Chicago, who in turn would report my confidences to the corrupt power brokers on whom I was blowing the whistle.

Finally, the time had come. I was down to the wire. I had hesitated so long to talk, and now, as I waited for Forstein and Beck, the strain seemed almost intolerable.

This was risky and probably pointless. I had no reason to think Washington could or would do battle with the tangled, organized forces of corruption in the city courts of Chicago.

That bleak afternoon in February, as I sat in the dim room, behind closed blinds, I asked myself some harsh questions. What did I really hope to accomplish? What were my true motives? I felt confused. I remembered when I sat behind a desk in a similar office in Nashville—the after-hours meetings we held there with government witnesses. Now the roles were reversed. I was not the prosecutor; I was the informant.

Was I just making a frustrated effort to recapture the excitement of those times? Those were good old days—when I still felt that with the forces of law and good behind me I could be the adversary of evil and make the good prevail—the days of Superman!

But now I wondered . . . and doubted.

Beck and Forstein finally appeared, and after meeting with them, I again felt confident I had made the right decision.

Beck was a take-charge man who asked all the questions. He was also gentle and encouraging. Forstein was the quiet intellectual type. He took notes.

They wanted me to meet immediately with representatives from the U.S. attorney's office in Chicago.

I refused.

The incumbent U.S. attorney, Tom Sullivan, was a Democrat and had both family and political ties to the Chicago Machine. Could he be honest—trustworthy? In addition, LeFevour claimed to be Sullivan's cousin. Maybe that was all political puff, but I was convinced that contacting his people would be dangerous.

Beck was extremely cautious, very considerate, and almost overly courteous and respectful. He obviously wanted to avoid pushing me too hard. He and Forstein changed tactics, suggesting that I contact Dan Reidy, one of Sullivan's assistants, and again I refused. I was later to learn, however, that Reidy, and perhaps even Sullivan, already knew of my anticorruption leanings.

Little had been resolved when I left after an hour, my parka hood again shielding my face. I tried to sneak out of the building, but a security officer at the only open door stopped me and told me to sign out. I was afraid not to use my real name in case he asked for identification, so I scrawled illegibly and hoped the Chicago police didn't decipher it.

I met Forstein and Beck again a few evenings later at the bar in the Pick Congress Hotel where Forstein was staying. It was a dark, old-fashioned room with the air of a Scottish castle, far from the territory of the fast traffic court crowd. Even so, I arrived early and surveyed the bar to make sure I knew no one there. Forstein and Beck found me at a small, brass-topped table in the room's farthest corner, well away from the patrons clustered around the main bar. After the amenities, Beck got down to business.

"Judge, as to your first concern, we have determined that there is federal jurisdiction."

"I'm not quite sure. On what basis did you come to that conclusion?"

"We feel that corruption within the court system affects interstate commerce," Forstein explained.

"Right!" I exclaimed. "Everything affects interstate commerce. But why are the Feds going to bother making a case on this sort of thing? What the hell difference does it make to Washington whether or not crooks are running the judicial system in Chicago?"

Forstein explained, "The Public Integrity section of the Justice Department takes the position that the public is entitled to expect their elected officials to give them a fair shake. We are willing to try to enforce that concept the best we can. And in most situations involving state or local corruption, we're the only game in town."

Beck continued, "What we're telling you is that we're interested, we think we've got jurisdiction, and we will try to do something about it if you help us."

Both men were treating me with such politeness that I felt a little foolish. I wondered at their confidence in me. They had not checked me out as far as I had been able to determine, and I wasn't sure how they decided I wasn't some kind of nut. When I asked them about this, they explained they were not going to make any inquiries because they didn't want to arouse unnecessary suspicions about me.

But I still wondered.

I also believed they were being unduly optimistic about the chances of Washington taking on the Chicago Machine. I made it clear that if they tried to use me for political purposes, or if I suspected they were, I would not hesitate to go to the media. They didn't appear concerned.

They wanted me to meet Woody Enderson, an FBI agent from Tennessee who had recently been assigned to the Chicago office. I agreed.

During my next two weeks on the bench in traffic court, I gathered a little more information while I waited to hear from the FBI. Tommie Kangalos told me LeFevour had been named presiding judge over all courts in the First Municipal District, which took in Chicago's Loop. This meant a great increase in LeFevour's power base. The judges who had been sitting in the major rooms in traffic court were now assigned throughout the system—and still paying rent to LeFevour.

I continued to pump Tommie for information, hinting that he was the most knowledgeable person in the area. As his ego inflated, it became easier to draw him out. I soon discovered just how easy it was. I had a date with a woman from downstate Illinois—a woman who had no contact with the Chicago court system. She met me at traffic court, and because I was late finishing that night, Tommie gallantly offered to escort her to a pub on Clark Street.

Tommie knew how to turn on the charm. He ran on bursts of energy, and when he was on a high, he bounded from woman to woman at a dizzying pace. With a new woman to impress, he was in his element. By the time I got to the pub, Tommie had corralled another judge (one of LeFevour's men), a public defender who was supposed to be one of Tommie's partners, and several other people from traffic court.

A deputy from the traffic court lockup was buying everyone drinks to celebrate his good fortune. He had been given the duty of searching prisoners, an occupation that apparently offered lucrative opportunities. According to Tommie, prisoners often "lost" things while they were being searched. Also, many were willing—and able—to offer their public caretakers substantial gifts, both monetary and sexual, in return for a well-placed word with the bond judge. Because the deputy who searches prisoners is one of the first officers that prisoners meet, he has the inside track on such payoffs.

The liquor was flowing freely, and, as was customary, Tommie had been tossing down Tanquerays-with-a-twist since noon. He was extremely talkative and obviously thought he was being particularly charming to my date. He maintained, loudly enough for the benefit of nearly everyone at the bar, that Judge Dan White (who had assumed LeFevour's former position) was just a figurehead.

"LeFevour is still pulling all the strings," Tommie roared.

He had another drink and proceeded to name several judges, bragging about "making whores of them," oblivious that his pronouncements were making the other judge in our party extremely uncomfortable.

Tommie told us all again (and again) about his greatest ambition. "Someday, I'm going to be the biggest and richest bagman in Chicago." The latest twist in this story, however, was Tommie's loudly stated desire to work directly for the King, Richard LeFevour. Tommie claimed that he was more reliable than the King's First Ward bagman, and that his job qualifications were better. I often wondered what those qualifications were.

With his usual lack of finesse, Tommie intimated several times that the judge with us at the bar was going to make a fortune in his new position—he was young, just beginning to go on the take. The judge

obviously didn't like Tommie's advertising, and he suddenly remembered an appointment at some distant location.

Tommie was convinced that he was making a favorable impression
on my conservative Republican girlfriend. He operated on the theory
that everyone was as impressed with a show of power as he was. He
would have been dumbfounded to realize how disgusted she was
with him and his cronies. Nevertheless, Tommie was a great source
of information. He kept me making notes constantly.

I still felt insecure about dealing with the FBI's Chicago office.
However, I finally met the FBI agent, Woody Enderson, late in March
while I was in Chicago to attend the Annual Associate Judges Convention. Check-in time was noon, so the morning was free for Enderson. I had already sent a summary of information to his home in
Tennessee.

It was a crisp, spring morning that March 25, and the sun was
shining. My spirits were high when we met in front of the ultra-
modern Continental Plaza Hotel. Enderson, accompanied by agent
Bill Megary, invited me into their car. We drove for some time, eventually parking in the drive leading to Adler Planetarium. Megary
seemed young, almost naive, but he was refreshingly enthusiastic
about the information I had. Already I was discovering that enthusiasm was an endangered emotion among these government-issue
types.

Megary did most of the talking, and I began to suspect the drawl-
ing Enderson was window dressing, the good cop gaining my confidence. Megary questioned me at length about everything I had written in the summary, almost as if he was cross-examining me in
court. He repeatedly pointed out instances where the evidence
wasn't sufficient to gain a conviction.

I began to think he was under the mistaken impression that I was
going to do his work for him. Hell, I was just pointing him in the
direction to go do his own hunting.

Against my better instincts, however, I agreed to help them start
the investigation. They told me it was absolutely necessary to get
corroboration of what I had been telling them in our taped conversations. I blindly agreed to wear a "wire," which I assumed was a

transmitting device about the size of a tie tack, that would link me to listening agents. (I had been watching too many spy movies.) I also agreed to introduce an undercover agent to the right people, but I adamantly refused to accept bribes or make a fix in order to help them tie down their case.

Megary embarked on a long discussion of the importance of secrecy. He told me my code name would be "Winston," and I should use it whenever I contacted Squad 17 at the FBI field office in Chicago. He promised that under no circumstances would his office advise the U.S. attorney's office about the investigation without first telling me. It would be several months before I discovered that the U.S. attorney's office already knew all about me.

Megary met me again, at the train station late on April 12, when I arrived from southern Illinois for my next stint in traffic court.

Once inside my apartment at River Plaza, he showed me the wire (a Nagra body recorder). I couldn't believe he really expected me to conceal it under my clothes. A Nagra body recorder is slightly smaller than a cigar box and about half as thick. It is substantially larger than the portable tape recorder Norelco makes for dictating, and much heavier. Its only apparent virtues were that I didn't have to plug it in, and it operated silently (powered by batteries) for eight hours.

Megary told me it could be held in place in the small of my back with a girdle contraption, which I disliked on sight. He assured me it was the only way to go. Although he conceded that a transmitter would be considerably more compact, he pointed out that the steel frames of Chicago's skyscrapers would interfere with transmissions.

As Megary talked, the implications of this operation suddenly struck me—like a bolt from a 220-volt line. I would be out there in the jungle all by myself. There wouldn't be any back-up agents. If I blew it, I was on my own, and God help me!

I woke up about five o'clock the next morning. Traffic court wouldn't open for four more hours, but I couldn't sleep. I fastened the girdle around my middle and tucked the recorder in place. Each microphone was taped to a shoulder, the wires taped in place along my body, and the whole setup covered with a loose-fitting shirt. I checked to make sure I could operate the on–off switch, which protruded through a hole in my pants pocket.

Megary dropped by a couple of hours later to check my appearance.

"Hey, Brock, you look great!" He smiled and patted me on the back. "Nothing shows. You just look like you put on a little weight."

He laughed, but I saw nothing humorous at all about the situation. As I trudged the three blocks to traffic court, I felt about as inconspicuous as a man in sixteenth-century armor.

When I walked into the building, Deputy Sheriff Elaine Dooley, wife of the former Chicago Bears' coach, greeted me with a warm hug. Elaine had been a Miss Florida, perhaps thirty years ago, and was still very attractive. That morning, however, she could have been the current Miss Universe and not increased my heart rate any more. As she hugged me, the body recorder seemed to balloon in size. I am convinced she took several years off my life with that friendly bear hug.

I hurried to get my assignment at Judge White's office and maintained a brisk pace until I reached my assigned chambers. I was relieved to find I was there before the bailiff. That morning I didn't want any help putting on my robe.

I sat behind the desk in chambers waiting for the first call, acting as nonchalant as possible. Only a few minutes had passed when I realized the girdle was cutting off the circulation to my legs.

"Oh, God!" I moaned. "What do I do now?"

Obviously, the unit was not designed for anyone who planned to be seated most of the day. Would I be able to walk after the first call? I wasn't sure my legs would support me if I stood.

Then Tommie burst into my chambers, all hyped up, and turned to close and lock the door. Imagining that he looked angry, I was on the verge of panic, but I managed to turn the recorder on.

Tommie took off his coat, exposing a .38-caliber pistol tucked in his belt. My heart was hammering, and I could barely breathe.

He walked to the window and looked out, then turned and focused on my phone. He took it apart and jabbed at its wiring, apparently searching for a bug.

I was almost ready to confess when he began to talk, almost jabbering. He was on one of his rolls—a high. He had been cheating on his taxes and kiting checks, and now he had smuggled an Uzi and 10,000 rounds of ammunition into the United States. A very busy young man!

"And to top it all off this morning," Tommie shouted, "this god-damn judge charged me fifty dollars to get a case continued. High-way robbery! It shouldn't have cost more than twenty-five dollars. I didn't make a dime."

I sat impassively as Tommie confessed to several federal violations unprompted by me. I prayed that the on switch was still on.

By the end of that tour on the bench, I was breathing easier and feeling more comfortable in my spy job. I believed I had collected enough information to confirm what I had told the FBI. I figured my secret agent days were over. How wrong I was. The next order of business was to introduce agents into the system.

Q: What was the nature of the agreement that
you entered into with the Department of Justice?

A: At that time, I agreed to record conversations
with an individual to confirm for the benefit of
the Justice Department some of the things that I
had told them previously. I agreed also that if
that was successful or if they decided to proceed
with an investigation, then I would be willing to
introduce an undercover agent into the system.

Vegas and Victor

My taste for excitement had been satisfied for the indefinite future,
and I was already looking forward to easing my way out of the operation. I anticipated a return to normalcy. I had verified the corruption.
It was time to begin introducing FBI agents into traffic court.

We needed a cover story, and David Ries, an undercover FBI agent,
flew into the Southern Illinois Airport near Carbondale on May 6,
1981, to help me invent one.

I was naively under the impression that the FBI was moving quickly. Later I was to discover that Ries, along with all the agents in Squad
17, had been involved for months as operatives in the Chicago investigation they called Operation Greylord. I had merely dropped myself
into their laps at the right time. They had needed a "Winston" for
weeks, and I fit their requirements exactly.

Ries, who took the code name "Victor," was to be set up in Chicago
as an attorney looking to make a fast buck. I liked Victor from the
start. We had a lot in common. He had been an undergraduate at
Southern Illinois University in Carbondale, and I had once taught
undergraduates there, so it seemed natural to introduce him as a
former student. We agreed that I would go to Chicago, ostensibly to
sell a race horse. Victor would pretend to help me with the sale, which
was to appear a little shady. Tommie Kangalos knew that I owned
race horses and that I had many friends and contacts among Chi-

cago's racing crowd. If Victor seemed to be involved in a questionable transaction, I believed he would win Tommie's confidence at once.

I called Tommie a couple of days later to make sure he would be in town and to tell him I would be there May 18 on business. I arrived at Union Station late on May 17 and met Bill Megary and Victor at the posh Palmer House, where they had arranged for me to stay. Tommie met me for coffee the next morning at New Mayor's Row, one of his favorite spots. I sketched out details of the sale and told him that a former student named Victor was going to help me out. Victor and I had planned to meet with Tommie at lunch, but Tommie had previous plans. He was free that evening, however, and we agreed to meet then.

After Tommie went back to court, I called Victor to change our approach. Our original plan had been to let Tommie see Victor hand me an envelope full of cash for which Victor already had signed a voucher. However, I didn't want to carry that much money around all day. I suggested that Megary ask a friendly banker for a deposit slip that would show a substantial sum. He agreed, with no objections. I hung up thinking that I was getting pretty good at handling people on both sides of this investigation.

I napped for a couple of hours that afternoon before Victor and I met. Megary had insisted that we eat before going out with Tommie. He was concerned that one of us might get drunk and blow the whole thing. It was obvious that Megary had never worked in the field. He didn't know how fear can keep a person sober. I had become used to working alone with the recorder and had confidence in my own abilities. But, because Victor was to do the taping that night, it would be a nerve-racking experience. He was so honest and straight-forward that I didn't know how he would fare with the characters who hung around with Tommie.

We met Tommie at Old Mayor's Row, an old-time restaurant off Mayor's Walk, just east of Daley Center. Every Chicago mayor, from the first to Jane Byrne, was immortalized in gold-framed pictures hung on the red brocade walls. Authentic bills announcing the closing of the place for violations of the national prohibition act in the 1920s were posted on the swinging doors that led to the Speakeasy Room. An open violin case fitted with a machine gun hung on one wall of the speakeasy, an almost campy reminder of Chicago's grim, not-too-distant past. And here it was that I had arranged a meeting between the figurative successors of Melvin Purvis and John Dillinger. I felt like the mysterious lady in the red dress.

We had a drink and met two of Tommie's friends. Like him, they seemed engrossed in making money and chasing women. Victor was uncomfortable, but he coped. After about an hour, we moved on to Hilary's in the fashionable Water Tower Place and met Paulie, one of Tommie's business partners. Paulie worked in the tort defense section of corporation counsel's office, and he and Tommie ran thousand-dollar scams with fictitious clients. Tommie would come up with a name, and Paulie would get authority to settle the fraudulent claim with the supposed client. Tommie would endorse with both his name and the fictitious client's name, then Paulie and Tommie would split the proceeds down the middle.

Paulie made me extremely uncomfortable. He kept patting me, offering to buy me drinks and set me up with two young girls who seemed to be his guests at the bar. He kept repeating that he appreciated the favor I had done him. I knew I had never done a favor for Paulie, and I figured that Tommie had probably sold me all over town with favors I didn't know about.

I noticed that Victor was trying to talk business with Tommie, and Tommie all but ignored him. I was afraid that Victor was pushing too hard, but by this time Tommie was well on his way to being drunk, so it really didn't matter. That night, Tommie was on one of his highs. He wore what he deemed to be the ultimate in fashionable attire—a Chesterfield coat and a white silk scarf. When he wasn't high, he usually forgot the scarf.

Tommie had once told me of his early efforts to be legitimate, but he had gotten into financial trouble and ended up divorced and in debt. He explained that by losing everything, he had learned the real value of money and power. He wanted to acquire wealth, which he had decided was the most important thing in the world.

"I don't care how I do it, by God," he repeated again and again, banging his fist on the table. "I kid you not—I'm going to be the richest bagman this town has ever seen."

The evening dragged on. We finally left Hilary's for a Rush Street bar where we met Rickie, who worked in the public defender's office. We hadn't been there long when we saw Gino Superchi making his way through the crowd. Tommie, ever vigilant for a chance to flaunt his influence, yelled for Gino to buy us a round. I didn't like the idea. I had no intention of crossing anyone who might have underworld connections, and I told Tommie I didn't want Gino buying drinks. I didn't know what he might expect in return. The First Ward people had a reputation for asking very big favors. Tommie laughed off my concern. Gino had an interest in the bar and could sign a tab for drinks. It was just like Las Vegas—the same type of operation— according to Tommie. I still didn't understand, but Tommie warmed to the topic. He pointed over the bar to an electronic board which displayed a running list of abbreviations and numbers.

"Do you know what that is?" he asked.

"Stock market results," I guessed.

Tommie was delighted by my ignorance. "You're a babe in the woods, Judge, but you're okay in my books. I'll soon teach you a few tricks of the trade."

He explained that the board was hooked into the "Chicago line," which gives bookies the odds on sporting events, both local and national. This fashionably appointed bar—hanging plants and all— was a headquarters for all the bookies on the North Side. Seated around the oval bar were various bookmakers, ready to do business with anyone who approached them. Tommie introduced one bookie, a man he identified only by his nickname, Racehorse. Racehorse and Rickie often made a threesome with Tommie on frequent trips to the Caribbean.

Gino Superchi dropped by our table a few minutes later and offered me another favor. Most of the girls at the bar were hookers, he said, and if I cared to indulge, I could do so as his guest.

All this information was great.Unfortunately, Victor was wearing the recorder that night, and no one was talking to him. Tommie simply had not warmed up to Victor. He either ignored him or, when forced to deal with him, acted disgusted or bored. After we left Gino's place, we had dinner and then stopped by another bar, staying until about midnight, when we finally called it a day. I was grateful that Victor had made it through the evening without being caught. I didn't think we had accomplished much or learned anything that could be used as hard evidence, but it was a start.

I reported my observations about Gino's operation to Megary and another agent the next morning and suggested that they tip off the Internal Revenue Service about Gino's bookmaking operation. They agreed it was a good idea, but they didn't follow through. In our breakfast discussion that morning, I learned that Dan Reidy, from the U.S. attorney's office, had known about me for a long time. Megary saw that this breach of confidence made me angry. He tried to placate me with assurances that my actual name had not been disclosed to Reidy—that Reidy knew me only by my code name.

"Ho-ho," I shot back at him. "I'll bet you still believe in Santa Claus too."

It was spring, 1981, my present Chicago court assignment was completed, and I was happy to head back to southern Illinois. On the train trip home, I thought about what I would do for a living in the future. If Operation Greylord continued until my involvement was exposed, would it be possible for me to pick up my life as a judge again? I doubted it.

But I believed that the commitment I made had been met. I had led the way; now the FBI could pick up the ball and run with it. I would go home and forget about the problems of Chicago. To hell with the whole thing! I intended to enjoy the summer with my kids in beautiful southern Illinois. I wasn't going to worry about the fact that Victor hadn't been accepted. I was done playing with fire. I knew how dangerous "show boating" was.

During that summer I found myself thinking often of a man named Ralph Brandon and how he would have loved to be in the spot I was in. Ralph had been a police detective in Carbondale, and he had entertained me and everyone else with his heroics and eccentricities. He was a small, athletic-looking man—no more than 5 feet, 6 inches tall, and weighing about 140 pounds. Like many small people, he made up for his size with a double helping of grit. Ralph craved excitement and tense confrontations. If he couldn't find any action, he would make some. In January 1976, Ralph had broken his biggest case. Two nights later, a friend called to tell me Ralph had killed himself.

It was then that I began to understand how little recognition some people receive for the work they do, and how big a price they often pay.

I speculated about how Ralph might have handled the situation in Chicago. He wouldn't have walked away and let LeFevour win. I felt that I was not measuring up to Ralph's standards of heroism. On the other hand, there were a lot of reasons to walk away, among them my young daughter Jessica and my recent involvement with Kathy. And I was going to quit the job as judge anyway. I really didn't care about it anymore. As a matter of fact, my continued association with the judiciary was embarrassing.

Besides thinking about my responsibilities at home, I kept telling myself that Victor could finish the job without me. There were certainly no guarantees that I could accomplish anything more by staying in the project; in fact, I really didn't expect that I would accomplish anything more. The system had existed too long to be changed. Besides, it wasn't my city and it wasn't my problem. I could ignore it.

For some crazy reason, though, I couldn't ignore it. Something kept nagging at me. If I quit now, I couldn't respect myself. I was afraid, but I knew what I had to do. I had known all along. Regardless of the cost, I felt compelled to proceed.

I didn't expect to be a hero. I didn't believe the public would care what happened. And I was sure the legal profession would be antagonistic toward my role in the operation. Nevertheless, I had to finish what I had started. As much as I hated to, I would postpone any attempts to live a normal life until I had made an honest effort to support the Greylord project to the end. That's just the way it was.

Q: As a result of those discussions, did you and the federal government eventually agree upon a new and additional role in which a new agreement with respect to your role in the investigation was reached?

A: Initially, at our first meeting in Chicago, we agreed that I would try to get into a major courtroom in the fall of 1981, that I would agree—I agreed that I would accept the full circuit's assignments so I would be up here almost continuously in the fall of 1981 for that purpose, to see if I could get into a major courtroom.

Dangling and Hanging

Bill Megary kept busy during the months of May and June 1981, trying to recruit me via telephone into a full-time assignment on the Chicago bench. He appealed to my professional instincts, and he appealed to my pride. He told me Greylord was terribly important, and the FBI needed my abilities and contacts. Megary suggested I might try introducing another agent as a labor union official, someone to whom Tommie might warm as a possible source of income.

Megary also appealed to another basic sentiment. He said the federal government wanted me enough to hire me—to pay me a salary. Perhaps that helped me justify, to myself, going back. If I was going to quit my job as a judge after this scam was completed, I was going to need money to fall back on until I found another career.

Giving up the judgeship was not a problem in some respects. I didn't really like the job most of the time. I did like the respect and prestige that the job carried, but the day-to-day work was tedious. There were exceptions. The big cases are always great, regardless of how a person is involved with them. But most of the routine matters were just tiresome. I spent long days on the bench, repeating defendants rights, over and over and over again, until I felt like a broken record.

On the other hand, leaving the bench scared me more than a little. Not many people go back into private practice after having been a judge. I didn't know how I would be accepted by either the public or the legal profession. When I accepted the judgeship, I gave up a stable law practice in Carbondale—one that had taken me ten years to establish. Those first years had been difficult, and I wondered if it was going to take another ten years to get back into the swing of things.

As an attorney, my primary income derived from representing defendants in criminal cases. Would I have any clients after having spent several years on the bench sentencing people to jail?

I thought about finding another profession, but I really wasn't qualified to do anything else—at least not anything that would bring in enough income to put my two older children through college. Every option I considered seemed to present insurmountable financial difficulties. I knew I had to quit—but I was really afraid to.

Megary asked me to think about what I should be paid if we made a deal with the Feds. After a day or two, I told him I thought the FBI should pay me as much as the state did, roughly $200 a day. Moreover, I would expect the agency to continue paying any extra expenses not covered by the state's per diem rate for visiting judges.

I calculated that, after taxes, I would take home about one hundred dollars a day. If I worked three to four months on the project, I should be able to collect about ten thousand dollars, enough to get me started in a new career. Megary didn't think my request would be any problem. He felt we needed to get together to work out the details, so I agreed to meet him and Dan Reidy, an assistant to the U.S. attorney in Chicago, on July 13, 1981, at the Midland Hotel. I thought I was all but hired.

To my surprise, Reidy was cool and aloof. Later, I grew to like and respect Reidy, but at that first meeting, I wasn't impressed. He acted as if I still had to prove my loyalty and ability to handle fieldwork. We didn't talk about money, mainly because Megary had led me to believe that part of our working relationship presented no problem. The discussion centered on whether I could get assigned to Chicago as a full-time judge. I assured them the other judges in my circuit would be happy to let me take on most of the circuit's obligation in Chicago—approximately forty-two weeks a year.

As far as being able to handle the field work, I knew I could fix almost any case in the city through contacts in traffic court. If Tommie couldn't handle a problem personally, certainly one of his partners, like Rickie or Paulie, could.

My main concern was that people would think I was crooked. What was I supposed to do if a real case came before me? I wanted federal authorization to handle that situation before I did anything. We agreed, I thought, that this authority would be forthcoming.

I also made it clear that I did not want to spend a lifetime in the city. I pledged myself to one year—no more. I also tried to make it clear I would bow out any time I lost my nerve or if I felt things were getting too dangerous, either for myself or my daughter, Jessica.

A two-week assignment in August was fast approaching. We agreed to postpone our new business relationship until that assignment was completed.

By the time of that July meeting at the Midland Hotel, I was starting to appreciate the significance of the overall project. I didn't know then that the Cook County states attorney and the chief presiding judge at the criminal division had requested federal assistance prior to my contacting the Justice Department. I also didn't know anything about an assistant states attorney named Terry Hake, who had also agreed to help with the investigation. As a matter of fact, I still didn't know the investigation had a name—Operation Greylord.

What I did realize was that Washington was taking judicial corruption in Chicago seriously. It became apparent during the meeting that realistic investigative procedures were being devised by the U.S. attorney's office, designed to prove that judges were actually taking money to fix cases.

I had never believed we would be able to prove in a criminal prosecution that judges were taking money. I had assumed only that if some bagmen were successfully prosecuted, it might serve to encourage the state to do some long-overdue housecleaning within the judicial ranks.

In a year spent worrying about solutions to judicial corruption, I had concluded the judicial system simply had no provisions for an effective self-policing program. Everyone had assumed the integrity of the system would remain intact. When this basic assumption was not fulfilled, the system had one hell of a problem.

No one wants to prosecute a judge. If the prosecution is not successful, then the prosecutor, rather than the judge, is in serious trouble. Even if the judge comes up dirty and investigators can prove their claims, they may be in serious trouble with other judges seeking to protect themselves. It is simply a no-win situation—one that everyone wishes to avoid.

In addition, before the Greylord investigation, no one had figured out how to investigate successfully a corrupt judge. Corrupt judges insulate their activities by using bagmen as intermediaries. They protect themselves in the same fashion that successful dope dealers do when they distribute narcotics. Like the dope dealers, only trusted associates are permitted to deal with the primary criminal.

When dealing with corrupt judges, the problem of insulation is further complicated by the fact that no immediately receivable product is being sold. With the dope dealer, at least there is an opportunity to catch him in possession or control of an illegal product. That opportunity does not exist with a corrupt judge.

Lenient judicial decisions can always be explained. Even the testimony of a bagman, indicating that he delivered money to a corrupt judge in return for a favorable decision, is in all likelihood not going to obtain a conviction. The judge will simply indicate that the bagman was rainmaking or simply guessing at what the decision might be when he took the money. Who is going to believe a bagman's word over a respected jurist's?

In the drug field it is customary to make cases on the intermediaries. They, in turn, are given the opportunity to "flip" or cooperate with the investigating authorities by making sales or picking up merchandise from their superiors. These transactions are recorded and observed, to be used as evidence in subsequent prosecution.

The same procedure could be used with regard to bagmen. I didn't believe the most serious judicial offenders would ever deal with newcomers like Victor or me. However, at the time of the Midland meeting in July 1981, the FBI and the U.S. attorney's office were taking the position that they did not want to make deals with bagmen. Later they were to become more realistic.

The most important aspect of the Midland meeting, as far as I was concerned, was to discuss a major obstacle to a successful investigation. In order to prosecute either bagmen or judges, cases must be available to market or fix. Unlike the usual narcotics investigation, where the undercover agent is merely buying an illegal product, the undercover agent in a judicial corruption case has to create the illegal product—a criminal case.

That is obviously a very big obstacle. The federal government did not want to fix real cases.

It would not have been hard to set up an undercover agent as a crooked attorney. He could have gone out and gotten crooked clients and fixed their cases, like all the other crooked lawyers in the Chicago system. However, that scenario presented serious problems regarding the Sixth Amendment rights of the defendant to counsel. That client might later complain that his rights had been violated. In addition, would the public believe the FBI was justified in getting actual criminals off the hook by paying federal taxes to corrupt judges to fix their cases?

At the Midland meeting, Reidy and Megary explained their solution. It was to create or contrive cases. Rather than prosecuting real criminals, FBI agents would act out illegal conduct for which they would be prosecuted. There were numerous difficulties with this solution which required false identities be created for each one of the agents involved.

There was also a very serious risk to those of us who had law licenses. Once the investigation was disclosed, the state supreme court could impose sanctions upon us for creating a fraud upon the court by knowingly presenting false testimony.

A few years before, an assistant states attorney from Cook County had been suspended for a year because he allowed false evidence to be presented in order to create a case against a crooked policeman. The Illinois Supreme Court had ruled, at that time, that the ends did not justify the means used in a successful prosecution.

All of us attorneys involved at the meeting were put on notice that our licenses might very well be in jeopardy at the end of the project. I was willing to accept that risk. I was far more concerned about having to fix real cases if I was forced to prove my trustworthiness to some of the bagmen.

In August I started my next two-week assignment, expecting to be authorized momentarily to fix real cases if it became necessary to protect myself. The plan was that I would set up several contrived cases the FBI was to have created over the summer, to be handled by the other judges.

In reality, it wasn't that easy to contrive cases. The Chicago police didn't like to arrest white, middle-class defendants, which most FBI agents so obviously were. The bureau, which has few minority members, did not want to use minority undercover agents for some reason.

In one instance, Ken Misner, a Squad 17 agent, made an extraordinary effort to get arrested for driving under the influence. He failed.

The scenario began when agent Jack Thorpe called the precinct to report a drunk driver, played by Misner. The pair waited quite a while, but no one showed up.

Thorpe called again. And again, nothing happened.

Finally, Misner decided to take matters into his own hands to get the attention of the police—one way or another. He wove his car across several lanes down to State Street, which is reserved for buses and taxicabs. He entered State Street, going the wrong way over two lanes of traffic.

A policeman finally stopped him. "Hey, buddy. The party's over. It's time for you to go on home."

Misner watched as the patrolman started to climb back into the squad car. Then, overcome by what appeared to be a drunken rage, he jumped out of his own car and climbed onto the hood of the squad car.

"You can't talk to me that way you ignorant pig! Who the hell do you think you are anyway?" Misner slurred the words as he apparently tried to focus on the surprised patrolman.

Watching from a distance, Thorpe wondered whether Misner had gone too far. No one is as tough or as deadly as a Chicago street officer—when he wants to be. Slowly, deliberately, the policeman approached Misner, grabbed his tie, and yanked him off the police car. An arrest seemed imminent.

The policeman filled out some paperwork and returned to the front of the car where Misner waited obediently. He handed Misner a ticket.

"Okay, buddy. I gave you a break and wrote you for disorderly conduct. The ticket is written for December 24 in the afternoon. The judge won't show up, so if you come to court, they'll throw out the ticket. Now go home and sleep this off."

Misner was too stunned to react. He watched as the policeman got into his squad car and drove off, leaving Misner behind the wheel, a very puzzled and disgusted FBI agent.

Another potential case fell through suddenly when the police got another call while transporting a "drunken" FBI agent to the station. The police officers simply stopped near a dark corner and pushed the agent into the street.

As a result of such mishaps, we had only one workable case prior to my arrival on the scene August 23, 1981. Woody Enderson had finally managed to finesse a driving-under-the-influence charge against himself. It wasn't a lot to work with.

When I got back to Chicago, I spent the next afternoon and evening with Tommie Kangalos. Tommie was up and ready to talk business. I just turned on the recorder and listened as he rolled along. He didn't need much encouragement after I told him I wasn't all that content at home and was thinking about relocating in Chicago.

"I really don't want to make a lot of money. I just need to make enough to get by—raise my kids and the whole deal," I explained to Tommie.

"I know what you mean," Tommie nodded vigorously. "There isn't any way you can get by in this world on the salary they pay us. Christ, I can't imagine how somebody with kids and all would do it. There isn't any way I could get by on what they pay me. My bar bill is more than most guys get paid in the system, you know." Tommie shrugged his shoulders.

"What I'm trying to find out is if I can work into this system up here—I mean that's an alternative," I said. "I can either go to work up here, on the side, or quit this damn job and go back to work in a law office downstate. But I can't get by on forty-five grand a year—there's just no way. I've got two kids who are going to be in college within the next few years. I'm not making it now and I don't know how I'm going to make it then."

I bought another round of drinks and continued. "I'm sure there's no way an outsider is going to fit in here—not for a long time. But I'd just like to find out if that's a possibility."

"You've come to the right man!" Tommie was all business now. I hoped the recorder was working properly. "I know everything and everybody—that's my business. How do you think I make so much money on the side around here? It's because I know who's who and what's what and what the freight is on everything," Tommie explained.

He held up his hand and crossed his fingers. "Richard LeFevour and I are like this—I mean really close. I don't know how much I've given that guy over the years, but I'm talking a lot of money. Do you know—do you have any idea—how much this guy makes? I'm talking like $400,000 at least. That's $400,000 without any taxes on it, man."

"I can't believe $400,000! There's no way he could make that," I responded.

"I'm telling you—it's like $400,000. This guy's got a cut of everything around here. The judges pay for the assignment and the bagmen pay to assign a judge. He's making money every time you turn around."

"Yeah, and all of his guys are hard-core Irishmen," I protested. "I couldn't fit into this system up here. He'd never trust me. My accent is all wrong."

"That's no problem." Tommie thrust his arms out for emphasis. He knocked over his glass but he kept right on talking. He'd had a smell of money. Money he could probably make off his new client—me!

"I can vouch for you," he boasted. "And like—you know—there's other guys in the system who would vouch for you. I think we could probably get you a spot. I know I could! You could probably clear $2,000 a week up here—even after paying rent to LeFevour."

It was my turn to sit up and show a little excitement. "Well let me tell you, if there's a spot like that around here, I'm definitely staying. You and I will live pretty good. We're going to cut a wide swath through this city!" I nudged him and winked. Tommie always liked that.

"You crack me up with that country boy shit," he laughed. "I don't even know what that means—but you still crack me up."

I pushed the point home. "I'm telling you, Tommie, if you set up a deal like that for me—whatever I get, 25 percent is yours."

Tommie was pleased. He kept smiling and patting me on the back. I hoped he couldn't feel the microphone wires taped to my shoulders. That's all I'd need right now.

It was finally time to make my big pitch. I took a long swallow of my drink and made a show of looking over the bar scene to make sure no one was listening.

"I do have a kind of half-ass idea for LeFevour," I whispered, leaning close to Tommie's ear. "It might do him some good for me to take the sensitive cases—you know, where the media might be looking at something like the deal the other day with Jane Byrne's daughter. It would have done him a lot of good to let a downstater handle that thing. I could take the blame for any problems and explain that I was just an uninformed country judge and didn't know what the hell I was doing. That way, King Richard wouldn't catch any heat over the deal, and we all get taken care of."

Tommie loved the idea. He said I could expect to double my illicit earnings. With this pitch, I let him try to persuade me. It was incredible how hard he was hustling.

I decided to send up a test balloon. Megary always talked about the need to get recordings with sex appeal for the people in Washington. In this case, sex appeal meant glamorous cases—the kind that catch the attention of the politicians and the press. As far as Megary was concerned, fixing parking tickets had no sex appeal. Fixing narcotics cases, murder cases, or arson cases did.

Tommie was getting drunk now, so I decided to try and get Megary something with sex appeal. "Tommie K., I got a deal for you, ole buddy, if you're big enough to handle it." I whispered the next words. "It'd be worth a ton of money if it could be pulled off. I'm not saying that you can do it. I don't know. I'm just wondering."

"I can handle anything, Brockie. What you got?" Again that pat on the back that always irritated the hell out of me—and at the same time scared me like the devil. I just knew that some day Tommie was going to feel those wires.

"This is a big deal, buddy. It's a chancery case involving an injunction. There are a couple of manufacturers and some big money. It's a technical case where franchise rights are being infringed. Anyway, the people who lost in the trial court—well, they need some help on appeal," I explained. Again, I looked around suspiciously to make sure no one was spying on us.

"Like, what kind of money is there in this deal?" Tommie's ears had raised a foot.

"Millions, I think. Lots and lots of money involved. What they are going to want to know is whether you can handle it, and I don't think it's going to stop at the appellate court. What do you think?"

Suddenly Tommie acted very sober. His response floored me.

"Yeah, I can handle it. It'll cost $100,000 plus 20 percent of that for me. The case has got to be good enough on appeal that at least one judge votes for it—legit, you know. All I can take care of is three votes. If three votes will get the majority opinion, then okay."

Seeming skeptical, I asked, "How do I know—or how do they know—they are going to get anything for their money?"

"You pick somebody to hold the money, and I'll guarantee it," Tommie assured me. "I'm saying they don't pay unless they get the result. Do you understand?"

I had no idea whether Tommie could carry out his boast. I hoped he couldn't. But knowing Tommie and seeing the way he reacted, I suspected he could produce. Megary would have to agree now that Tommie's statements had produced a lot of sex appeal. Megary agreed all right. His smile was a foot wide.

It was another two days before I talked to Tommie again, but he opened our discussion where we had left off. He wanted to talk to LeFevour and get some guarantees.

Things were suddenly going a little too fast. Washington had not authorized us to fix any real cases. I was beginning to think I might be tested any minute, and I was afraid of what might happen if I didn't pass the exam.

Jack Thorpe dropped by my apartment early the next morning to pick up the tape of that conversation with Tommie. I told him I wouldn't record anything else until Washington gave me an authorization to proceed. I was getting in deep water now—and it gave me a shiver or two. Jack pleaded with me to continue, but I walked out on him.

As a result, I wasn't wearing a recorder when Tommie and I discussed fixing the only case we had—Woody Enderson's drink case, which we had begun to set up sometime before. Woody had posed as my friend and as a racehorse owner. His supposed trainer had contacted me for some help.

When I brought the matter up with Tommie, he indicated it would cost Woody $1,000, $400 of which was to be my referral fee. An attorney friend of Tommie's would get $100 for acting as defense lawyer. Tommie would give the officer maybe $50 and the clerk $10, and he would keep the rest for himself. It sounded as if I would be the only one making much money. That puzzled me, but I let it ride for the moment.

I was having trouble getting Tommie and Woody together, mainly because the FBI hadn't yet set up any phone numbers that were not answered "FBI." Woody wasn't having any luck trying to reach Tommie by phone. Finally, Woody rented a motel room near the track and waited there one day until I got Tommie to call him.

The contact went off without a hitch. I heard two versions of the way the case went down.

Tommie was pleased with himself. "Man, your friend was really impressed. He never saw anything happen like that. I was just in there wheelin' and dealin' and telling him what was going on and everything. Like, he just couldn't believe how I could handle the whole system."

"Did you treat him okay?" I asked.

"Yeah, he's like—you know, a really nice guy. He's all right—talks just like you do," Tommie laughed.

Later, I heard Woody's version. "The fool's in there explaining to me how the whole thing works—how it's all crooked—how he's a prosecutor and not supposed to do anything like this. And I'm recording the whole conversation."

I responded, "You probably didn't even have to ask. He just wanted to tell you how big a deal he was. Right?"

"Right! That's our boy," Woody smiled.

Later that same afternoon, I met again with a group of assistant U.S. attorneys for a pep talk at the Midland Hotel, a favorite undercover meeting spot. Their assurances about the great job I was doing left me untouched. I felt I was getting a snow job and I told them I didn't give a damn about their praise or about Washington's problems with making decisions. What I did care about was getting authorization to proceed. I was a sitting duck and I didn't like it. I told them I was quitting until I had that authorization. Before we moved any further, I wanted my ass covered.

I was scared and I didn't mind admitting it. Also, I was damned angry that official protection for me was so slow in coming.

"Damned bureaucrats," I muttered as I walked out and closed the door behind me.

The next day Tommie met Woody, who was wearing a body recorder, and told him everything was taken care of. Woody paid Tommie the $1,000.

We had a case!

That afternoon I kept away from Tommie. I wanted to avoid accepting a fee on a contrived case. I was willing to continue helping out, but I wasn't going to end up in jail and have all the big shots in Washington forget they knew me. I was not going to put the wire back on until I was protected. And I certainly was not going to receive any money without official authorization.

On my way home that weekend I felt angry and isolated. No one in the Washington FBI hierarchy seemed to give a damn about the help I was giving them. There was no one I could trust anymore. All the king's horses and all the king's men and all of Kathy's efforts couldn't put me back together that weekend.

In retrospect, I feel all the lying and deceit were beginning to take their toll on me. I hadn't been trained to handle it. A policeman friend once told me, "The FBI will promise anything and follow through on little or nothing. Beware of them."

I was going to do just that!

On the Monday following that angry, unhappy weekend, I met with Megary in Chicago. He was apologetic when he explained that I had been misled. The bureau had had authorization to fix real cases from Operation Greylord's beginning. He told me Victor had been working on the project at least a year before I became involved. What's more, the Cook County state's attorney, Richard J. Daley, was cooperating.

This information really frightened me. What other information were they holding back on me? How many other people knew I was involved with Greylord?

After the 1980 election, Daley became the state's attorney. He had been sworn in by the judge of his choice, Judge Richard LeFevour. Ira Blackwood had told me long ago that LeFevour was godfather to one of Rich Daley's kids.

From the start, everyone in Greylord had promised they would not tell Daley anything without warning me ahead of time. Now, I discovered that Daley knew about me before I even met Megary.

I was sick with rage and fear.

Megary's assurances that Daley didn't know my real name—only my code name—just made me angrier. Realistically, how many downstate judges could be in a position to know the things I knew? It would not take the targets of the investigation ten minutes to figure out who Winston was—to know who was supplying all the information.

It is hard to describe the bitterness I felt as Megary made it clear how consistently they had deceived me—"for a purpose," he pointed out—while I was risking my neck. He was genuinely embarrassed, but, at the moment, I hated his guts. Much later, when I was finally rid of the fear that had gnawed at me, I came to admire Megary.

Finally—with reservations—I put the recorder back on that afternoon. I rationalized my decision. I was in so deep now, what the hell did it matter? It occurred to me later that Megary probably figured I would feel that way. Very tricky!

The next morning I had coffee with Tommie, and he handed over one hundred dollars as my referral fee on Woody's case. He was supposed to pay me four hundred but, for our purposes, the amount didn't matter.

I had finally crossed over the line. If I ended up in prison, I had no one to blame but myself. I couldn't wait until evening to get rid of the money.

I called Squad 17 and arranged for Thorpe to meet me early. Thorpe and Misner compared the serial numbers of the bills I had received from Tommie to those Woody had given Tommie. They matched. We had a good case, and we had proof of my ability to infiltrate the system. I assumed we finally were ready to make me official. I should have been happy, but I was too numb.

After my two-week assignment in Chicago, I returned to Marion on September 8, wondering if I had lost my sanity, getting so deeply involved with Greylord. There seemed to be some compulsion to stay involved. I began making arrangements to assume the circuit's remaining assignments in Chicago.

In order to take over the entire circuit's assignments, I had to do a little explaining. I talked it over with the chief circuit judge, and, to be on the safe side, explained what I was doing to three of my closest friends who were also judges.

Then I sat down and wrote out a summary of my involvement with the FBI. For safekeeping, I gave it to a police officer from Carbondale, who was also a friend. The hardest thing was to try to explain to Kathy what I was doing, without alarming her.

I told everyone else that I was earning credit for future years in Chicago by spending a substantial amount of time up there while Jessica was not yet in school. I had to come up with a good excuse for being there because, previously, I had complained bitterly about the nature of the Chicago assignments. In order to remove any doubt about the authenticity of my desire to spend forty-two weeks a year in the city, I claimed that I had been promised an assignment handling felony jury cases if I came to Chicago on a continuous basis.

My confusion and doubts about Greylord mounted when Megary called to say the FBI was having second thoughts about paying what I had asked for. There apparently had been some discussion about paying me one hundred dollars per day, tax free. This would have been roughly equivalent to my original proposal.

However, Megary assured me that everything had been worked out, and the FBI's undercover operations committee had approved the entire project in principle.

By the time I returned to Chicago, on September 25, Megary had changed his tune. The project was still up in the air, and no payments had been authorized. But he did assure me that everything would be worked out shortly.

Days went by. I felt rebellious and resentful when Megary told me a Washington-based supervisor, Dana Caro, wanted to check me out. I was in no mood for more tests of my loyalty. A promise had been made to me, and now that promise was not being kept. Worse yet, I was still floating around in this dangerous game with no official, written authorization.

Another meeting was arranged for October 6 at the Midland Hotel—again to discuss payments and written authorization for me to proceed. As usual, it coincided with my lunch hour. Missing meals was becoming commonplace. Before Greylord was over, I would lose twenty pounds.

Victor and I arrived early. As the others arrived, we trickled upstairs to the suite, consciously ignoring each other. Misner and a clerk named Nancy stepped into the elevator with Victor and me. Nancy didn't know either of us by sight and seemed surprised when Misner introduced us. She had expected us to look different, somehow. I thought I knew what she so politely avoided saying. I was sure that anyone who heard the tapes would expect me to look sleazy.

I was embarrassed to think that someone who looked as young and naive as Nancy had been transcribing the conversations I had taped. Much of the dialogue, especially if it involved Tommie Kangalos, degenerated to the level of an adolescent boys' locker room. In order to ingratiate myself, I had resurrected every war story I could think of. While these stories seemed to appeal to Tommie's crowd, I doubted that someone like Nancy would find them very attractive.

The meeting room filled shortly with perhaps six or seven local agents, Nancy, Victor, and me, plus the two Washington representatives, Bob Walsh, Megary's contact in Washington, and his supervisor, Deputy Director Dana Caro.

Megary had been under pressure for some time. Apparently he hoped this face-to-face meeting might placate Washington on one side, and Victor and me on the other. It might also help him solve some of the bureaucratic problems that had plagued us for weeks.

I did not feel particularly placated myself. How unnecessary all this was, and how potentially dangerous to the project. Victor and I didn't need all this attention. It seemed to be nothing more than a dog and pony show for Washington, and Victor and I were the stars of the show, a dubious honor at best. However, I tried to be pleasant out of consideration for Megary.

Walsh seemed to be an unoffensive, down-to-earth person, but like the rest of us, he answered to Caro.

Caro was a relatively small man, not over 5 feet, 6 inches tall, and weighing maybe 150 pounds. His ego transcended his physical limits. No one could remain uncertain for long that he viewed himself and his position as extremely important.

Caro discussed various aspects of Greylord with me, touching on some of the key factors and the possible political ramifications in both Chicago and Washington. It was obvious he was preoccupied by the eventual public reaction to our investigative techniques.

Greylord was unprecedented, and because it followed so closely on the heels of Abscam, an earlier, somewhat similar operation in Washington, FBI officials probably were concerned about a congressional backlash.

Nevertheless, I felt belittled by comparisons Caro drew between me and Mel Weinstein, the man who not only masterminded Abscam for the FBI, but who made a lot of money and escaped criminal prosecution in the process.

I wasn't too dim to realize that my efforts to shake the federal money tree had somehow soured my relationship with the FBI. But what everyone seemed to forget was that the FBI had approached me with an offer to pay—not vice versa. Now they were trying to back off, and I sure as hell didn't like the way they were attempting to renege on what I thought was their deal.

I understood the pressures on Megary and Caro, but right then I was more concerned with my position than I was with any heat they might be getting. After promising both protection and money, Washington was now leaving me dangling and unprotected. I had been flirting for weeks with some pretty rough characters. It was my right now to expect my position would be pinned down—in writing.

The worst of it was that we weren't getting anywhere in solving the problem. The bureaucrats, like Caro, had to decide whether to jump into the project with both feet or get out. I sensed that Caro was nervous about moving off safe middle ground.

Probably no area of the law is so scrupulously avoided by law enforcement officers as public corruption, and for that I blame the politicians. Often, antitrust violations or other white-collar crimes are not pursued because that would mean an attack on many who underwrite political campaigns.

But the root of the problem is that to attack public corruption is almost certainly to attack elected public servants. And until Abscam—the congressional bribery cases—that just hadn't been done on a large scale. The significance of Abscam was that the FBI broke with tradition and ignored the political consequences of targeting Congress.

Caro was concerned that Congress might be looking for a chance to get even. Operation Greylord might give it the excuse it wanted to cut the bureau's budget. He was also concerned that the judiciary of the nation's third largest city might be too sacred a cow to sacrifice.

Caro dominated the group's general discussion. He assured me that the bureau had been impressed with my efforts, my courage, and my sacrifice. It was the same speech I had been hearing for months.

Then Caro added a touch of drama to his performance. He leaned forward and looked me directly in the eyes. "Is there anything in your past that would embarrass the bureau?"

I couldn't restrain a laugh. The whole thing seemed ludicrous. I glanced at Victor and saw he agreed. I wanted a minute to respond.

"No. Before I started hanging around with these guys, I had a pretty good reputation. Now that's shot all to hell," I said.

Everyone laughed.

"I've been divorced twice," I added. "You might make a note of that."

"What would your former wives tell us about you?" Caro asked.

"Well, we got along pretty well. Probably they'd say that I'm a pretty good father and a not so very good husband. Maybe I'm a workaholic. I don't know. I have no objections to your asking them."

"Anything else?"

"Not that I can think of," I said in all sincerity.

Caro paused and studied his hands. "What do you want to get out of this anyway? Are you going to run for office?"

I replied, "No."

"You know this could make you attorney general of Illinois or something?" he insisted.

"No. I'm certainly not going to run for any office." It was my turn to be emphatic now.

"Then what? Do you want to write a book or something?" His tone was menacing.

I wondered if he had been taught to use that frightening voice or if it just came natural to him.

I shrugged. Then I thought, "Maybe I should."

It is ironic, in retrospect, that his sarcasm about writing a book is probably what got me started. As soon as he said it, I thought he was probably right.

The meeting finally ended, and I rushed back to court. Unkept promises were still unkept.

Q: Approximately when did you begin to wear the concealed tape recorder?

A: In April of 1981.

7

Wired for Business

Almost every morning the alarm rattled me awake at 5:30, when it was still dark outside. Some nights it seemed as if I had just gone to sleep when it was time to get up again. A raucous group always left the Candy Shop, a strip joint around the corner, around the time I was trying to doze off. And usually I heard the crowd leaving Rush Street at two o'clock. These late nights and early mornings were killing me. But I had to get up—there was no time to waste.

Worse, I was always thinking, planning, and worrying—mostly worrying. It was fall of 1981, and I was still recording. Living with the wire had become an all-consuming project. Concealing the body recorder was a particular problem because I had to take my jacket off at work. If I put the recorder in the middle of my back, the way most people wore it, it would be obvious to anyone who happened to be around when I took off my coat or put on my robe.

Because of the difficulties, we decided to try a new approach. I would attach the unit to my leg and conceal it by wearing cowboy boots. The country-western fad was sweeping the city, so many people up and down Rush Street were wearing western boots with their three-piece suits. I thought they looked ridiculous, but I decided boots might provide a safer way to cover up the recorder. Besides, they matched the accent I had cultivated to fit my image.

Ultimately, however, I discovered that by using a larger girdle I could lower the recorder so that it would fit in place near my hip pocket, where my billfold normally would have been. The recorder was larger than a billfold, but not much, so it really wasn't noticeable. By then I had lost twenty pounds, and the recorder fit comfortably into my too-big pants.

The life of a spy bears no resemblance to the glamorous adventures depicted in James Bond movies. My duties seemed extremely dull and tedious 99 percent of the time; the other 1 percent was filled with terror.

I also paid a high price in loneliness during this period in my life, although the FBI agents never seemed to understand this. Taping assignments always seemed to interfere with what I wanted to do—to go to the sauna, to go to the Merchandise Mart to try on clothes, or to go have a drink with a lady—a friend of someone in the building that I "had to meet." Usually, at the last minute, I would just make an excuse. If it had to be really good, the excuse would be Marie Dyson, my FBI "date," who would show up unexpectedly. I had no real social life. Marie accompanied me to dinners or to parties that we thought might be good hunting grounds. It was difficult to get close to anyone while I wore the wire.

This sacrifice was really brought home to me the day a traffic court deputy named Debbie asked me to lunch. Debbie was one of the most beautiful women I had ever met. She wore custom-tailored linen uniforms, and came to work every day looking like a million dollars. The day she asked me to lunch, I thought, "Wow! Maybe all these James Bond fantasies are coming true." Sadly, I discovered that Debbie was interested in me only because of my position. After that, I knew I had to steer clear of any further social contacts with Debbie or anyone else. Close social involvements might be dangerous, and I might compromise the assignment by allowing anyone to get close to me. My isolation increased.

The FBI provided me with all the recording equipment and technical support I needed to get the job done, and they continually improved the equipment. I began with a mono-microphone recording device and finished with stereo. Then they added the car. The "batmobile" was a late-model Chrysler that had been seized by drug enforcement agents in New York and transferred to the FBI for use in Operation Greylord. Before I got it, it was equipped with four microphones in the roof and an on—off switch in the door handle. I never used this rather elaborate recording device, but I knew it was there if I needed it. I was also issued a spy-novel piece of equipment to carry a recorder in—an attaché case with a false bottom, microphones hidden in the hardware, and an on–off switch where the lock would have been.

But the Nagra recorder continued to be my workhorse. I spent hours taping, with the Nagra on my hip. I developed the habit of daily talks with courthouse people about activities within the judicial system. I tried to find out what was going on not only in traffic court, but in other branches of the court as well. I tried to obtain as much detailed background as I possibly could.

In order to avoid the problems raised by entrapment—suggesting criminal activities to people, rather than just finding out about them—I always made an effort not to say much. I would begin to say something, and then I would let the other people fill in the blanks. In other words, I developed the habit of stammering and pausing throughout a conversation. I noticed on the tapes that my accent, a southern drawl, became more pronounced as time went on. I was afraid that before the project was over I would sound like country music star Mel Tillis. Maybe I did.

Frequently, there were technical difficulties with the recording equipment. Sometimes the microphones didn't pick up, and on a couple of occasions, the tape stuck in the lid when I closed it. The on–off switch, which was located in my pocket, often did not operate; and if I happened to be seated when the conversation began, I had to be a bit of a contortionist to turn the equipment on. There just wasn't room in my pants pocket to determine accurately the position of the switch. If I wasn't sure, I would excuse myself and go to the bathroom, turn the recorder on, and come back. By that time, any conversation that should have been recorded might be over.

I was told that recording these conversations was necessary. Criminal cases had been prosecuted for years without tape recordings, but now, to avoid any possibility that a jury might not believe a prosecution witness, recordings are often used in court proceedings.

Although in the Greylord case there were volumes of recordings, only those tapes considered most important were transcribed to be used by the prosecution. It is very difficult to transcribe a recording because, frequently, more than two people are talking. It is critical to make sure that the speaker can be identified in each instance. Many times, the person transcribing a tape will be confused about who the speaker is, and the undercover agent ends up being credited with all the incriminating statements. To avoid this problem, I would read each transcript after one of the agents assigned to the case had reviewed it. Later, the transcripts were read by the assistant U.S. attorney, and then he and I reviewed them again before trial. The amount of time spent in transcribing and reviewing the tape recordings probably approached fifteen to twenty times the original recording time. I was never sure that all of this effort was worthwhile.

At first I doubted whether the risk of detection inherent in using a recorder was offset by the benefits. Eventually, however, the recorder did give me some sense of security. It recorded what I was doing—and what I wasn't doing. It also gave me control over the FBI. If things didn't move through bureaucratic channels quickly enough, or if I didn't get the necessary backup for a project, I simply quit recording. After that, things moved along quite rapidly. Even so, my relationship with the bureau remained tense, chiefly in the areas of my credibility and my billfold.

By November 2, the problems of "no money and no written authorization to proceed" came to a head again. Megary tried to let me down easy. He wanted me to meet U.S. Attorney Dan Webb for the first time. I knew by Megary's voice that something wasn't quite right.

It turned out that FBI Director William Webster had decided not to pay me anything. He expected me to work for nothing—to be a good citizen. And I still had no written authorization to protect me if I had to handle a real case.

I was furious! This was not what I had been promised. If they hadn't wanted to follow through, why had they made those promises when they recruited me? I felt I was being manipulated, and I sure as hell didn't like it. It was my neck on the block—not theirs.

Megary urged me to meet Webb and, considering the circumstances, the meeting came off well. Megary had warned me that Webb looked awfully young but that he was a good man, in his mid-thirties. Megary was right on both counts. Webb looked about twenty-two years old. I figured his appearance must be a real drawback in his position as U.S. attorney for the city of Chicago.

Webb had a wealth of assets to make up for his youthful looks. He was intelligent, articulate, and a hard worker. He listened well, and he had the ability to gain one's confidence quickly. Unlike most political figures, he was not afraid to take a chance.

I liked Webb right off the bat and I felt he was probably a talented trial lawyer. He had credibility, or believability, a quality that makes a difference with a jury.

He struck me as honest and competent, self-assured without being too cocky. I was relieved and somewhat revived. Maybe Operation Greylord would be a success after all.

Webb explained the problem we were confronted with. "It all boils down to this. The director has reservations about paying a judge."

The FBI was still burning from criticism for paying exorbitant fees to Abscam witnesses. Webster didn't want to get burned again.

Webb asked me if a single $12,000 payment at the project's end would satisfy me. I wasn't sure. What if I worked only two or three more weeks and the project blew up or I got scared and quit? Webb assured me that would be their worry, not mine. I accepted the arrangement.

Webb worked on the bureau over the next three days, and Washington finally responded on November 5 with a decision that the FBI would pay only "reasonable relocation expenses."

I was flabbergasted and told Webb to forget the whole damn mess. Unless they were going to specify the amount I would be paid and my exact status—in writing—I wasn't going to make any deals with the bureau.

I didn't trust any of them anymore. "And I'm not signing any agreement," I added emphatically to Webb, "unless you co-sign it. I've been pushed around and dangled in the air long enough."

Webb smiled briefly. "I think it's time for you to meet the director— face to face."

WINSTON: You know what Ira's good at. He
can . . . he can fake like he's joking but, uh, find
out what your reaction is to almost anything
without sticking his neck out at all.

> KANGALOS: I'll tell ya something. He's got a pretty
> good position there. You know, he's . . . he's
> directly wired to the deputy chief. That's his
> man.

8

Ira

It is time for me to tell you more about Ira Blackwood, the police
officer who had asked me to do a favor for an IRS agent—a friend of
Judge Richard LeFevour. I have tended to ignore Ira thus far in this
story, and I ignored and avoided him for the first several months of
Greylord.

An outsider might think Ira was an oddity—a renegade or a rebel.
Years later, Assistant U.S. Attorney John Newman was to describe
him as totally incorrigible.

But Ira was my friend, and I had a certain respect for him.

Officially, Ira was a policeman. But he was more than that—much,
much more. At first glance, he seemed a simple man, without any
particular substance. Closer inspection proved him to be an extremely complex individual.

Though he was fifteen years my senior, he and I understood each
other in a way few people do. He was a man's man, but in no sense the
type of egotistical, insecure fellow that phrase usually describes.

At fifty years of age, Ira was physically awesome, a solid 190 pounds
spread over a stocky five-foot, ten-inch frame. He looked the image of
what he was—a former professional boxer with a young man's body
and reflexes. Ira could run three or four miles when he felt like it, and
he lifted weights and practiced karate just for fun. He was a natural
athlete and possessed the strength and stamina of a man who was in
training continually. Ira looked and acted a lot like Charles Bron-

son—handsomer perhaps, but with that haggard, seen-it-all Bronson look.

Women were attracted to Ira and he was certainly no woman hater, but as far as he was concerned, women simply didn't compare to men as companions. He treated women politely enough—made sure they got home safely and occasionally held a door open—but I can't imagine Ira ever choosing a woman for a friend.

I always felt that Ira was a product of the system in which he lived. A better system would have produced a better product. In order to understand Ira, it is necessary to understand the system. Like so many policemen, Ira was courageous, brutal, and cynical. He had seen it all. He had learned to take care of himself—to survive.

Unlike most of the other people I met in Chicago, Ira and I spoke the same language.

His southern Missouri background was much like mine, but we shared more than the same culture. We had in common a broad variety of interests. Though streetwise and adventuresome, his interests ranged from women to horses, and included politics, religion, art, sports, and philosophy. He was unceasingly curious about life and could enjoy and converse as easily with a priest as he could a Mafia lord, an artist, highly regarded jurists, successful attorneys, and those who weren't so affluent.

Ira and I had good talks, ate good food, had good drinks, and saw good plays together. He liked to go first class, but I doubt anyone ever saw this backwoods Missourian display any social affectations.

Ira relied on inner strength and security, the equal of which I had known before only in an old Indian who lived off the land back home. Maybe Ira drew his confidence from his Irish-Indian genes, too—or perhaps it was conditioning from an extremely rugged early environment.

Ira claimed that his father had been an enforcer for Al Capone, an irony that he, as a Chicago police officer, loved. The elder Blackwood moved his family from southern Missouri to Chicago when Ira was still small. This career move eventually landed Ira's father in Alcatraz, on a federal conviction. Ira claims Capone offered the president of the United States a million dollars to pardon his enforcer, but the president turned him down after the Bureau of Prisons and the U.S.

Department of Justice said the elder Blackwood was "too incorrigible."

Meanwhile, Ira grew up on mean streets, playing with the Irish and Italian kids who were to prove so influential later in his life.

Ira liked people as much as I do. Though he was a brutal man with more than his share of prejudices, he could be amazingly sensitive to people's needs and moods. As much as I loathed and feared his excesses, on a personal level I liked and admired many of his character traits. He was loyal and reliable. He genuinely enjoyed helping most people.

When the city of Marion was devastated by a tornado on Memorial Day weekend in 1982, Ira was the first one who called to see if I was all right after phone service was restored. I've never forgotten that act of thoughtfulness.

Perhaps my closest bond with Ira was his job. I had been a police officer while working on my political science degree at Oberlin College and again for a summer during law school at York Beach, Maine. Later on, I had been chairman of my home town's police and fire commission, and in my private practice I represented police officers in several civil and criminal proceedings. I roomed with the city's assistant chief of police after my first divorce, and I still have several close friends who are policemen.

Occasionally, police work can be intoxicating. Police officers know the sensation of wielding immense power, even the power of life and death. But they know more intimately the dulling boredom of the routine patrol.

The police so often see people at their worst—an occupational hazard. They have a real cynicism about the rest of humanity, and it is not based upon race, color, or religion. Often they lack respect for those outside their profession. Unfortunately, it's often easy for police officers to go one step further and include themselves in that group. Policemen can become very self-destructive. Most drink; some do worse.

I found Ira refreshing, for he was a long-time cop who still thought well of himself. With some exceptions, he also had a good opinion of the rest of the world.

Ira and I met through another downstate judge, Charles Quindry, with whom I had dealt occasionally as an attorney. I was in my first stint in traffic court in the fall of 1979. Quindry, an associate judge in the circuit neighboring mine, was serving his third or fourth year on the bench. He already knew several people in the traffic court building, so after we made contact, he introduced me around.

When he invited me to join some of his friends for drinks after dinner one night, I accepted with alacrity. Our other two drinking companions were a full circuit judge from Quindry's circuit and Ira.

Ira took us to a quiet bar called the Pipeline, just a block south of the traffic court building, on Clark Street. We sat at the end of the bar, talking about the difference between Chicago politics and downstate politics. We found out that after years of paying his political dues, Ira had come up for a political job. He had been slated to run as a Republican candidate for the Illinois General Assembly.

Ira, of course, was no Republican, but the Democratic machine had enough registered Republicans in its ranks to nominate and elect a candidate in the other camp. The party faithful had no qualms about voting for whomever the party told them to, whether they were registered Republicans or Democrats. This strategem gave them an inside track on everything going on in the opposition's caucuses in Springfield—a good political trick. Normally, it would have been a simple matter to get Ira elected, but Ira's regular Republican opponent challenged his petitions. Apparently, many of the names had been forged by a lazy worker. Ira decided to withdraw graciously.

We had a couple of drinks at the bar and, to our discomfort, Ira insisted on buying every round. It was obvious he was a regular patron. It also was obvious he was a close friend of the barmaid. Ira introduced us, and we settled into easy conversation. The bar wasn't busy, and the barmaid didn't have much to do other than keep us supplied with fresh drinks.

Before long, I realized that a well-dressed elderly man, two or three seats to my left, was trying to attract my attention. He was smiling loosely and making a determined effort to focus on his surroundings as he lifted his glass to us—or maybe just to me. I couldn't be sure at first. I finally got his drift when he mouthed the words,"I love you," and blew kisses my way.

I turned to Ira, on my right, to fill him in on the man's conduct. I laughed and joked about the man being so drunk he couldn't tell who he was making a pass at.

But Ira couldn't see the humor. He watched the man a few moments, his face hardening. He told us the man was a housing inspector. Then he said, ominously, "You fucking queer; get the hell out of here."

The old man just kept smiling his blurry smile and raised his glass again, toasting me. Furious, Ira slid off the bar stool and began to move toward the oblivious drunk. I stepped off my stool and grabbed Ira. I knew he could walk through two of me if he wanted, and I was thankful when he chose not to. The incident shook all of us.

The barmaid begged Ira to calm himself, and Quindry suggested we try another bar. Ira agreed and told the barmaid to get her coat and come along.

She smiled ruefully and said she couldn't leave for another half hour. But Ira wasn't to be denied. He demanded that she tell her boss she was going with him. However, the boss refused to make an exception; if he let her off early, everybody else would want off, too.

Ira's rage was re-ignited. Working to control his voice, he began softly, "Did you tell him it was me asking?"

As the barmaid answered affirmatively, her boss started toward us.

Casually, he said, "I'm sorry, Ira, but I can't. . . ."

"This place is fuckin' closed, you asshole. Do you hear me?" Ira emphasized every word.

The boss tried to protest, but Ira didn't give him a chance.

"I said it's closed." He spit out the words. "I never asked for nothing before, you son of a bitch. You are shut down."

Ira turned and walked out. We all followed, three downstate judges of the law feeling somewhat awkward at being accessories to such a curious bar brawl. The next time I heard about the Pipeline, it had been closed. And it never reopened.

That was the first incident that made me suspect Ira wielded a great deal more influence than the average Chicago cop.

Quindry tried to lighten the atmosphere, suggesting we hit a bar near his hotel. Ira objected, saying he didn't have a sponsor there.

"What's a sponsor?" I had to ask.

Ira explained that he enjoyed certain arrangements at several bars, including the one we had just left, that allowed him to buy drinks on someone's tab. Apparently the money he handed the barmaid was being returned to him as change. I told him it was our turn to buy.

We walked into the next bar, which was long on customers and short on waitresses. We found a table in the back, and I went to the bar to order a round. As I turned away with four drinks on a tray, a little man suddenly rounded the bar and knocked all the drinks to the floor. He spoke nothing but French, but he was able to express his embarrassment and to apologize by buying us a double round and helping me carry the drinks to the table.

None of the others had witnessed my mishap, so as I approached the table, I put my arm around the Frenchman and said, "Hey, Ira, I got us a sponsor."

Everybody but Ira laughed.

"Who is this guy? Where is he from?" Ira demanded. This was all very serious to him.

Ira and I began to spend a lot of time together after that, my first spring in Chicago. But it took me nearly nine months to begin to appreciate his stature in the system.

Ira wielded much more authority throughout the traffic court building than his rank as a patrolman seemed to warrant. I suspected his job supervising court officers in the building must be political—hardly an uncommon situation.

For a long time, I thought Ira Blackwood was basically a good cop with, perhaps, a few sidelines it was better to know nothing about. I assumed he marketed favors along with everyone else, and I was aware he had asked fellow police officers to kill cases for high-level politicians. That was, indeed, part of his operation—but only a small part.

In many ways, Ira was just another Chicago cop. Chicago policemen tend to be rather intimidating people—big and reasonably athletic.

The brutality of the street life they witness often seems to instill within them a coldness. They seem to operate on a different, more primitive level, and they have a look about them that reflects neither fear nor compassion. Veterans with battle experience sometimes have that same look.

These street policemen, with whom I spent considerable time in Chicago, seemed to share a general frustration with the system— with both the judges and the juries. As they viewed the situation, it was almost impossible for them to get convictions, for one reason or another.

The more I observed the system, the better I came to understand this rotten judicial corruption.

In some cases, jurors tended to be afraid of the defendants, especially if they were gang members or gang-related. In a typical trial, many "brothers" sat in the courtroom, and their presence seemed to create a "reasonable doubt" as to the guilt of the defendant. In other cases, defendants with money or connections seemed to walk away from their legal problems. Quite naturally, policemen were frustrated.

This frustration frequently led to conduct that was understandable but less than professional. Often police officers would engage in punishments known as street adjustments.

Most street adjustments probably happened to minority members who never complained. People who believe they are part of the white-collar establishment are most irate when they encounter such conduct. A few of their stories are worth repeating.

One story I heard involved a businessman out for an evening walk. He came upon two men, fighting at the edge of the street. Being a large man, he stepped between the two and held them apart. When the police arrived and asked what had happened, the businessman told them he did not want to be involved, and he started to walk on down the sidewalk. Words were exchanged between the police and the businessman.

One thing led to another, and the police threw the man in the paddy wagon which had arrived at the scene. The businessman rode around, locked in the back of the paddy wagon with drunks, hookers, and what have you. When his fellow passengers were let out at the police station, he was detained. Finally, after ten or twelve hours in the paddy wagon, he was released in the middle of a neighborhood that was unfamiliar to him. The police turned him out and left him standing on the sidewalk.

So much for the lesson of not getting involved.

In another case, an accountant with a fairly lucrative downtown firm went to Rush Street after work with several friends. They had a few drinks, and he walked out of the bar by himself, to go home. He stopped a moment in front of an alley, trying to figure out where he had left his automobile parked. A stranger stepped up and asked if he wanted some dope. The accountant responded that he certainly did not, and he started to move on.

"How about a woman?" the stranger asked.

The accountant responded that he was not interested, and he tried to move away. The stranger grabbed him by the tie, swung him into the alley, and struck him in the face with a gun.

The accountant pleaded, "What do you want?"

The assailant responded, "Give me all your money—everything in your pockets." In his haste, the accountant did exactly that, gave him everything, including his billfold, change, and car keys.

The assailant then struck the accountant again and ran off down the street.

The accountant, with blood running down his face, screamed for help. Everyone on the sidewalk strolled on by, staring at him.

Finally, a passerby told him there was a police station three blocks away. The accountant ran to the police station and burst in on the desk sergeant, who was reading the evening paper.

"I've been robbed!"

The sergeant responded, "So? What do you want me to do about it?"

The accountant said, "What do you mean? You're supposed to go catch the thief!"

The bored sergeant asked, "Do you know who robbed you?"

The accountant's fear turned to anger. "Hell, no, you idiot! You're supposed to go find out who robbed me!"

The sergeant just kept reading the newspaper.

In a rage by now, the accountant screamed, "I demand that you do something!"

The sergeant calmly put down his newspaper, took the accountant's name, and left for a few minutes. When he returned, he advised the accountant that he had two parking tickets outstanding and that twenty dollar bonds were required on each ticket. He refused to allow the accountant to call the suburbs, a long distance call.

Since the accountant could not make a phone call and had no money to post bond, he spent the night in jail. He might have been there still except for the fact that the commander on the next shift loaned him a quarter to make a collect phone call to his wife.

I am sure the accountant felt he had suffered a great injustice, but he didn't know what suffering really was.

One day I ran into an attorney-bagman who hung around the traffic court building. His face was so swollen and discolored that I didn't recognize him, even when he took his glasses off. He looked as if he'd gone through the windshield of a car.

His speech was hard to understand because he couldn't move his lips or jaw. Nevertheless, he finally managed to explain what had happened. He had had a run-in with the Chicago police. His version and the policeman's were somewhat different, but they both agreed that he had tried to fight with a patrolman and had lost the battle.

According to the officers' story, they had tried to stop the bagman for a traffic violation. Instead of stopping, he took off. There was a high-speed chase which ended at a bar. Sure that he was carrying some kind of contraband, the police chased him into the bar, where he ran into the bathroom. The policeman assumed it was to flush the contraband down the toilet.

Angered because they had been unsuccessful in stopping the disposal of the contraband, the policemen decided to teach the bagman a lesson. Despite his power and influence in the system, they beat the man unconscious, fracturing numerous bones in his face during the process. His influence would later get him out of the traffic charges, but that did not prevent the serious injuries he sustained.

Although many Chicago policemen are intimidating individuals, one deserves particular mention. He is "Popeye Doyle" of the Chicago police department. (Popeye Doyle was a famous New York detective in the French Connection.) I had only one experience with the man, but that was enough to make me believe the numerous stories about him.

This officer, whose real name I've forgotten, was seated in the front row of my courtroom one morning, wearing blue jeans and a leather jacket. He looked like a truck driver. He had a stocky frame and was about forty years of age. Because the first row of seats is reserved for police officers, I thought someone had made a mistake and the bailiff just hadn't noticed. I didn't realize he was a police officer.

I had an extremely light call that morning and there were only a few casual stragglers coming in, mostly one at a time.

A black youth, about nineteen years old, was called up to the front of the courtroom. He was sullen and hostile about the proceedings. He had some minor violation and, after hearing the facts of the case, I sent him to Room 19 to look at the movie.

When I announced my decision, the defendant responded by saying, "Oh, man."

Suddenly the truck-driver type jumped up, grabbed the defendant by the throat, and made him stand up on his tiptoes. "That's not 'man,' it's 'Your Honor, sir!' Do you understand me?"

Both the youth and I were stunned. The youth apologized while I sat and stared. I wondered who this character was.

When I stepped off the bench to take a break, he came back and introduced himself as a police officer. Popeye Doyle apologized for his conduct and left.

After that I heard several stories about his adventures. Perhaps the most descriptive concerned his return to street duty after being on sick leave for some time. Popeye had been stabbed in the side of the head, leaving a hole about the size of a quarter in his skull, just above the temple. Having a soft spot like that is very dangerous, especially for someone like Popeye.

When he returned to work, he was naturally assigned to a desk job, but eventually he got himself reassigned to street duty. Popeye was required to take a rookie along. This was intended to cramp his style and perhaps keep him out of trouble. But Popeye had different ideas.

During his first night back on the beat, determined to establish his presence, he parked in front of a pool hall, then he walked up to the door and kicked it in rather than open it.

Popeye grabbed the closest man by the hair and jerked him backwards across the pool table, causing him to open his mouth as he was stretched backwards. Popeye pulled out his trademark, a sawed-off, double-barrel, twelve-gauge, chrome-plated shotgun with a pistol grip. He cocked both barrels and stuck them into the pool player's mouth.

"Now, get everything out and on the bar," he ordered.

The patrons emptied their pockets. Knives and guns appeared on the bar. The rookie, who was still trying to fix the door, was ordered to pick up the weapons. Then he and Popeye beat a fast retreat out the door.

"Tell your friends that Popeye is back in town," the burly policeman roared.

During our brief encounter, Popeye explained the philosophy of life by which he lived.

"If they think you're afraid of them, you're dead," he replied.

I thought about that several times later.

It would be easy to criticize the police for their actions, but somehow I can't feel too critical toward them. In the whole scope of things, their abuses seem the less severe. Certainly, the public has to bear some of the responsibility for the ways in which these men respond to the violence around them. I cannot help believing that street adjustments are a by-product of a faltering, corrupt legal system.

Ira was, perhaps, typical of Chicago policemen, but he was also very different from them—and different from anyone else I ever met.

I liked him, feared him, and respected him. And I didn't want him involved in Operation Greylord.

Beyond a few personality conflicts, which were essentially minor, my main complaint about the FBI's people is that they didn't know how to relate to a citizen witness.

I suppose that this experience was as new for them as it was for me. Normally, FBI informants are either criminals working off a penalty or people being paid to provide information. Under both of those circumstances, the witness is an outsider to the bureau and is treated as such.

All sorts of things emphasized the distance between the FBI agents and myself. For instance, if I asked questions about any of the people being investigated, I seldom got an answer. I was told that information was given out on a "need to know" basis, and the agents rarely thought I needed to know. My role was simply to give them information.

Occasionally the U.S. attorney's office would give me some indication as to where the investigation was headed and what the principals were looking for. Other than that, I worked in the dark.

Megary was obviously embarrassed one day when he slipped and mentioned the name Operation Greylord. For the first time, I learned that the project had a name.

As soon as Megary said the words he realized I hadn't heard them before. He quickly explained he was not authorized to reveal that information, and he asked that I not mention it. I promised I wouldn't, but I wondered what the hell difference it made.

I mention it now simply to illustrate my relationship to the bureau, a relationship that continually made me feel like an outsider, and a mentally inferior one at that.

Perhaps if I had been made to feel a part of the prosecution team, I wouldn't have gotten so close to Ira. I don't know. What I do know is that, at the time, I was experiencing some real misgivings about my job. I mentioned this fact frequently to the agents, but they did not seem to understand and would cut me off when I brought it up.

In contrast, Ira was always concerned and interested. I needed someone to talk to, and during the week he was the only one available. So, as much as I hated doing it, I frequently confided in Ira (although, of course, not about Greylord). On the weekends, I could talk out my frustrations with Kathy, my real-life girlfriend. Without her understanding and support, I don't know what I would have done.

Unfortunately, I couldn't talk to either Ira or Kathy about the things that really bothered me. I discussed with Kathy my feelings about the FBI, but I didn't mention how dangerous Ira or the First Ward people were. I tried to make her think I was simply dealing with a bunch of old, incompetent, drunken judges.

But, sometimes, I just felt desperate to talk freely to somebody on the inside so that I didn't constantly have to be on guard. The agents never gave me that chance, which contributed to my hostility toward them.

I had always found Tommie to be obnoxious and a serious threat, but I had deluded myself into thinking that Ira was basically a pretty good guy. However, one day I sat in the safety of a motel room, three hundred fifty miles from Chicago, and listened to tape recordings in which Ira, Tommie, and I discussed various scams to screw everyone but ourselves. I realized then that Ira was not a good person. In fact, he was a dangerous psychopath and as despicable as anyone I had ever met. I was shocked by the emotional rapport I had developed with that man.

Several years ago, F. Lee Bailey attempted to defend Patty Hearst by describing her emotional condition as being typical of that of a hostage. Although the concept of the hostage syndrome has attracted a good deal of attention since then, our understanding of it is still vague. Nevertheless, there is some general comprehension that hostages or captives frequently align themselves emotionally with their captors, rather than with the police. Apparently, some underlying psychological factor correlates survival with affiliation with the original enemy, rather than with the police. The captives fear they will be killed if the police interfere. As a result, they become more afraid of the police than of their captors.

I do not understand this process, but I may have experienced it in my relationship with Ira. The thought struck me that perhaps my fear of Ira had somehow caused me to align myself with him rather than with the people in the FBI. I may have ignored Ira's faults in order to avoid dealing with my fear of him. It was a frightening idea.

After a few weeks of wearing the body recorder, I believed I could avoid discovery by targets of the investigation only as long as my identity was not disclosed by some federal bureaucrat.

This fear of betrayal was constant and prevailing. A recurring nightmare plagued me two or three nights a week in which I died as the result of a Chicago gangland-style killing. Just before I awakened each time I always wondered who had screwed up and gotten me killed.

Because of my experience, I began to wonder how many undercover agents burn out simply because they have no way to deal with their fears and self-doubts while they're in the field. I suspect it is a substantial number.

Ignoring the stress of undercover work results in a substantial waste of manpower. It is similar to running a young horse, week in and week out, without giving him time to recover or "freshen up" between races. A good horse won't last a year without rest. He'll just quit trying.

Undercover agents without a means of emotional release seem to last about the same time. They quit trying or they turn bad, which represents the ultimate alienation from the office crowd.

And some, in a final act of desperation and isolation, kill themselves.

I do not believe that the inappropriate affiliation I developed with Ira entirely explains my antagonism toward the FBI.

Part of it was caused by the agents' behavior toward me. And I believe my feelings were justified.

TOMMIE: Tell me what it is, what the pay is. Okay. But here's the problem with the fucker. There's a civil suit we got, right. A $150,000 insurance fraud scheme, the (garbled) insurance company are not payin'. (Garbled) . . . what I need from you in the case is (garbled). . . . what I need is a directed verdict but I can't come out and say it. . . . All right, I don't give a fuck.

9

Into the Mire

From the very beginning of the operation, my number-one target was Richard F. LeFevour—The King. All the corruption seemed to ooze down from him.

I thought, initially, that Tommie Kangalos would be the best avenue to get to him. We hoped that through Tommie I would be placed in a lucrative courtroom, for which I would pay rent to LeFevour. The potential to obtain solid evidence was mind-boggling.

Tommie seemed confident that he could get me appointed to a major room as long as I was willing to play ball. As it turned out, Tommie wasn't nearly as big in the system as he had claimed. Apparently it takes years to establish the reputation needed to earn a place in a gold-mine courtroom. I didn't have years to spend. We kept getting the runaround from LeFevour and his people about putting me in a "good" room. Meanwhile I was gaining confidence in my ability to handle Tommie and to wear a wire successfully. But I was not at all prepared for the next development—Ira Blackwood!

Evidence of Ira's involvement came to my attention so abruptly I was stunned. I had supposed that Woody Enderson's contrived case was really a test—a test of whether or not I would take a payoff. The deal had been made and the FBI had paid Tommie to take care of Woody's case. I had never suspected, however, that there was a "business relationship" between Ira and Tommie. I hadn't asked many questions about Ira, mainly because I didn't want him to turn up dirty. I didn't care about Tommie.

By October, however, I was forced to come to terms with Ira's standing in the system. Tommie always had been full of bluster about his power and influence, but it finally became clear that he was still at the bottom, while Ira had achieved management level.

I tried to avoid Tommie after he took Woody's payoff for handling the bogus case. I still didn't have authorization to fix any real cases, and I refused to accept money without authorization. Again, I hounded Megary to push my official papers through fast.

I got the same old answer from him. "They'll be here any time."

One day Tommie invited me to go to have coffee, and Ira "just happened" to show up. Ira and I were sitting next to each other in a booth, and Tommie was sitting across from us. The restaurant was full of morning coffee drinkers. Tommie pulled one hundred dollars from his pocket, threw it on the table, and told me to take it.

In that instant I was placed on center stage, front. Ira watched me closely—stone faced, silent, waiting.

I was shocked that Tommie would throw money around like that in public. But most of all, I didn't want Ira involved in this transaction. I said I didn't want the money, and I pushed it back toward Tommie.

Now Ira inserted himself into the deal. He laughed. "Never pass up the money."

I picked up the bills and slid them into my coat pocket. I felt like a man going down in quicksand. At the same time, Ira threw a wad of money across the table to Tommie.

His voice was commanding. "That's the C's money."

I knew that signified the Chief or LeFevour.

I tried to keep track as Tommie counted out LeFevour's share of the money. I had a hard time concentrating. I was sweating blood. Later, I heard thirteen sounds on the tape as Tommie counted the money.

I knew Ira had too much money for a cop, but I just kept hoping he wouldn't get involved in Greylord. He hadn't been a target, so far, and I supposed he would be ignored along with dozens of other minor scam runners who pervaded the building. We couldn't haul in everybody.

But now, Ira had made himself a target—and in my presence. It made me sick to involve him. He was no minor player in this game, either. He had shown me he was a biggie. I knew now that Ira would have to fall, and for one reason only—because he knew me. I would be the one who had to trap him. That hurt!

There can be no other aspect of law enforcement as emotionally draining as undercover detection, but until I implicated Ira, I hadn't fully appreciated the difficulties.

The defendants are never some far-removed bad guys. They are people you get to know and like; they have families and they are not much different from anyone else.

I had much more in common with Ira than I did with those aloof agents who sat in their offices and contacted me at regular intervals for tapes and information.

It might seem incredible that anyone could like a man who so calmly talked of brutalizing and killing people. I hated that part of him, myself. But Victor and I both liked Ira, the person, to Megary's disgust. When I discovered Ira was bad, I felt as if I had lost my only real ally.

My new business relationship with Ira brought on a personal crisis. Until then, I had been confident that if Operation Greylord and my cover blew up, I could count on Ira to get me out alive. I didn't have that kind of confidence in the FBI. I was painfully aware that implicating Ira was a significant step forward for the project, and I should have been happy about that. Instead I was very depressed when I learned that Ira was involved. I couldn't shake it from my mind for several days.

Right away, I tried to talk the FBI into letting Ira flip. But the deeper we got into it, the less they thought they could honor my request. Ira was too high up in the system. He was one of the biggest fish they had. A lot farther down the line, I finally convinced Webb that anyone who was a bagman, as opposed to a judge, ought to be given the opportunity to cooperate.

Looking back, I know Ira was at that table, having coffee at that particular time, to see whether I would take Tommie's money. That was the first step in getting him to vouch for me with LeFevour. In the topsy-turvy world of judicial corruption, Ira was a bigger figure than Tommie, despite the fact that Tommie was prosecutor in city court. It seemed incredible that a patrolman could wield more power than a city attorney, but Ira went back a long way with a lot of influential people. Most important, he had proved that he could be trusted.

Ira was the most powerful bagman I met during the time I was in the city. To be a successful bagman, you have to be able to talk directly to a judge. Ira could talk to all of them, mostly because he had been assigned as a supervising officer in traffic court for years, and he met all the judges as soon as they were put on the bench.

It's hard for outsiders to understand the significance of a bagman. In order for a case to be handled on its merits, you need a good lawyer. If you're going to fix a case, you need a good bagman. It's that simple. After Woody's payoff, I had the opportunity to watch a good bagman—Ira—in action on many occasions.

On one occasion, Tommie was representing a Greek restaurant owner who had torched his place of business. This was happening all over the city as the economic problems of the late seventies made insurance fraud commonplace. Either because of his age or his inexperience, the old Greek had not gotten clear of the building when it exploded. He was found unconscious in a pile of rubble, traces of the accelerant still on his hands and coat.

Tommie and Ira discussed the case in my presence. Now that I was a trusted judge who was on the take they talked openly. Tommie wanted to know whether Ira knew the judge who was handling the case. Ira indicated that he did.

"Can you give me a hand with the Greek?" Tommie asked.

Ira nodded. "Sure. No problem."

Then he added, confidently, "We'll give him supervision."

Ira and Tommie grinned. I tried to smile.

Arson is a Class X felony and requires six years in the penitentiary. However, Ira was sure that he could get the judge to reduce the charges and give the man a probationary sentence which would not appear on his record.

Tommie wasn't satisfied. He explained that there was an insurance policy of $150,000 on the building. If the man was convicted of anything, he would not receive the proceeds of the policy.

"We've got to have a 'not guilty' finding," Tommie insisted.

"No problem," Ira agreed. "But you've got to give the judge something to hang his hat on."

Tommie nodded and said he would have one of his partners "step up" on the case. He would give him some kind of bizarre theory on which the judge could find the defendant not guilty.

"How much will the freight be?" Tommie asked.

"A dime apiece," Ira replied with no hesitation. "A dime for you; a dime for me; and a dime for the judge."

Being an outsider, I could get away with asking. "What's a dime?"

Ira explained. "A thousand dollars."

I really couldn't believe it, and I told him so.

"You mean to tell me that you're going to do this case for a total of $3,000 and the man is going to make $150,000?"

Ira nodded. "You gotta learn not to get greedy, Judge. We don't get rich on one case. Just take a little—it's safer that way."

"Yeah, I guess you're right, Ira."

As they worked out the solution, I was recording and pondering what else the government would need to know to make the case. I figured we would have no problem identifying the judge from Tommie and Ira's conversation, but I was less confident of the client's multi-syllable name.

Tommie mentioned it several times, but I was afraid the recorder would garble it. I broke into their conversation, and asked, "How do you spell that name?"

Tommie spelled it without pausing.

I shook my head and joked, "It's all Greek to me."

Tommie went on discussing the case with no suspicions. Later, when Victor was listening to the tapes, he couldn't believe my brashness in asking for the spelling.

Neither could I.

Ira handled cases all over the city. He got bunches of tickets from the mayor's office and from the police department on a regular basis. Most of these fixes were political favors. Ira would make a call to the judge and explain what the defendant's connection was. The judge would just pitch the cases as a political favor. If any money was involved, Ira never failed to divvy up among the judge and the various people involved. He was an honest man in that respect. In fact, he had the best reputation for "honesty" of all the bagmen I encountered.

It wasn't long before I found out that one of Ira's major clients was the First Ward—the Mafia area. He took to lunch with him on several occasions "Uncle Ben" Mincelli*, the man who brought him the traffic tickets for the First Ward. Those lunches were like something out of a movie. When Uncle Ben appeared in the restaurant, everyone bowed and scraped. He never seemed to pay for anything. I don't believe a bill was ever presented. Perhaps the cost of having your restaurant financed by the Mafia was to "feed" them any time they wanted to be "fed."

Ira told me that one time—years ago—he had a very big decision to make: go into the Mafia or into the police department. He decided that the police department was a better money maker.

Though he chose the relatively straight life, he kept his contacts with organized crime, which gave him ties to some of the most powerful people in the city. Ira also had powerful connections with police and political patrons. One of his mentors held a very high position in the police department—a man named Beckwith.* Ira characterized Beckwith as "one mean motherfucker."

"He has fifteen to twenty official kills," Ira added with great pride.

"What's an official kill?" I asked.

"You know, where we write it up." Ira smiled.

Ira also enjoyed the benefits of coming from park district superintendent Ed Kelly's district. Kelly was one of the last surviving powers from the Forty-seventh Ward, and he was a solid party member who refereed battles between the First Ward and the Byrne and Daley forces.

Kelly's considerable clout made life a little easier for all his "boys." People from his district got good jobs in the system. As a result, Ira got the job he wanted.

Ira and I frequently talked about his past. He told me about some of the things he had done during his career. He always had a knack for making a lot of extra spending money. But like he said—he never got

*Pseudonym.

greedy. A fair price was always charged for his services. Customers always left happy.

Ira didn't have many scruples about augmenting his police salary. His conscience stretched quite easily. He sold real estate on the side. He also sold silver, which he processed from x-ray photographs he and a partner collected from hospitals all over the city. He had been on the take as a street cop, turning a nice profit from restaurateurs willing to pay to avoid trouble over unlicensed parking lots.

Ira avoided the usual scams of charging ten dollars to get off speeding tickets in favor of charging restaurant and bar owners one hundred dollars per month (plus drinks) for an illegal parking lot.

Somewhat more ingenious was the practice he engaged in, while on the street, of writing up accident reports for the benefit of a prominent lawyer. Ira explained that he would assess the situation when he arrived at the scene and make arrangements for the person who appeared to be most seriously injured to get in contact with that attorney. Then he would write up an accident report that would make the other driver responsible.

"I tell ya, Brock," Ira said, "I could get $2,500 up front for a good case like that. One of those a month was all I needed."

Ira's philosophy was to take money only on serious cases. The rest were freebies. Little scams were never worth the effort. Ira deadpanned, "Don't insult me with $20, I tell my customers — $200 maybe, but not a lousy $20 bill."

Ira made sure his friends worked. Several attorneys in the traffic court building had been put there by Ira. One fellow I met, an attorney who had hit bottom, was so unreliable that Ira couldn't depend on him most of the time. He would decide the pressure was too much, or he didn't want to handle something, so he would go jogging or go talk philosophy with somebody until three o'clock in the morning. Ira still kept him on, helping him out. He kept the man busy running errands and keeping his car washed. Ira also tried to find him a place to live and tried to keep him out of trouble with his ex-wife for not paying child support.

There were probably three or four attorneys Ira had put in a position to make $100,000 or more a year. They'd never charge Ira anything for "stepping up" on a case. "Stepping up" means having an attorney who knows about the fix appear with the client in court so the deal can be concluded by the judge. Ira could always count on these attorneys, and if he got a good fee, he would pay them.

Ira handled things the same way for the police and the politicians. He'd take people under his wing and give them a chance to get on their feet again. If they turned out to be unreliable, he'd drop them and go on to somebody else.

Ira never quit this kind of activity. He continued to be a regular attorney referral center, steering all sorts of cases—from divorce cases, to real estate transactions, to criminal cases—toward attorneys willing to pay for the service.

Ira once told me if I could swing a pending multi-million-dollar downstate divorce case to a lawyer he knew, he could guarantee me a $25,000 referral fee. I passed that one by.

As far as I know, Ira never had the opportunity to follow one pursuit many Chicago police officers found to be an easy assignment with lots of benefits and prestige—acting as a personal bodyguard. These policemen, paid by city taxpayers, are assigned to protect dignitaries within the city and are dished out like so many other favors to the city's chosen few. I never quite understood how this system works, but the bodyguards seem to function as chauffeurs and errand boys for celebrities. Winning the services of a personal bodyguard was a true indication of rank in Chicago.

Knowing who sponors these bodyguards and how they are distributed can provide a key to understanding political affiliations in the city. For instance when a policeman with ties to the heavily Democratic First Ward was assigned to Republican mayoral candidate Bernard Epton in the spring of 1983, insiders knew the Italian power brokers were not going to back black Democrat Harold Washington.

One night Ira talked about being on patrol with a man who later became personal bodyguard to Ray Meyer, the very successful coach of the DePaul University basketball team at that time. Ira said he and the other patrolman "really pulled some shit."

On one occasion, they saw a homosexual walking down the street, and they rolled him for a couple of hundred dollars. Later that evening, they saw the same man out again, and Ira's partner said, "Let's do him again—you know—see if he went home and got a new bank-roll." So they rolled the man again. That time they got around four hundred dollars.

As he recounted the story, Ira laughed until tears came to his eyes. "The guy is screaming that the cops were robbing him. And we're telling people walking by, 'Man, this guy is bananas, you know.'"

I drank a lot of coffee with Ira and learned much in the process. Although not a very talkative person, he did give me many interesting insights to the city and its politics, and he reminisced occasionally about his past.

After high school, Ira went into the Army. He indicated that he had had a lot of disciplinary problems as a result of his unwillingness to submit to authority. He used power one way or another, avoided it, or ignored it—but he never bowed to it. I suppose that's one reason why I liked him. He was one of the few people who would stand up to Richard LeFevour.

While serving in Korea, Ira was promoted to the rank of sergeant. He was placed in charge of one portion of a POW camp, where the prisoners burned him in effigy. He explained that he had "warned the little slant-eyed bastards" that "if they fucked around with me, they were dead!" They thought he was bluffing—or maybe they couldn't understand English. He didn't know. Whatever, he took twenty of them out on a work detail, and they never came back.

"Nobody really gave a shit," he shrugged. "It was, you know, war and all that."

The day Ira told me about the POW camp, he got caught up in talking about violence. Ira had been a semi-professional boxer and could handle himself without any help, but he was inclined to use whatever means he could to give himself an additional advantage.

He described beating a man in the face with handcuffs until he had nearly killed him. He explained that he had brutalized the man in front of a big crowd of people so he could establish his authority in the area he was working.

"I broke all the bones in his face. Hurt him real bad," Ira told me, speaking as casually as if he were giving me the time of day.

Ira admitted that a lot of brutality charges had been filed against him over the years.

He told me about the time he ran a barbecue skewer through a man's chest at a picnic. Ira had warned him not to mess around with him, and when he didn't heed the warning, Ira just stuck the skewer right through him.

"He didn't die, so nobody cared."

Again, a casual shrug of the shoulders. His tone of voice sent cold chills up my back.

On one occasion, a black man stabbed Ira's partner. "He cut him pretty bad—eighty stitches." Ira chased the assailant across town to a second-story apartment where he kicked down the door and walked in with his gun drawn. The black man fell to his knees and dropped his knife, giving up.

Ira barked, "That's not the way its done, motherfucker," and he grabbed the man by the hair and threw him out the window.

"My God, what happened?" I thought perhaps the man had died as a result of being thrown from the window.

Ira continued. "I went down and stomped the shit out of him."

Miraculously, all the victims, except the Koreans, had lived. I hoped I would be so lucky. . . .

Despite the coffee, my mouth was dry as dust. I didn't have to wait for the FBI to verify what Ira was telling me. He wasn't a boastful man. He wasn't even trying to be entertaining.

He was just reminiscing.

Q: With reference to the investigation, what did
Officer Blackwood say at that time?

> A: He told me that there were big problems, that
> he, Tony Bertucca, and Judge McCollom had just
> been summoned from the traffic court building
> over to Judge LeFevour's office. They were told
> there that there was a news, television news,
> crew doing an exposé or investigation of traffic,
> the traffic court building. He told me that the
> three people, McCollom, Bertucca, and Ira, had
> been told to flatten the building for sixty days,
> meaning stop any illegal activities within the
> building. He said it was a bad time to come up,
> that he didn't know—he didn't think—I could
> make any money coming up at that time.

10

A Spy Behind Every Bush

Once I began to see how much influence Ira Blackwood had with
various power brokers in Chicago, I figured it was just a matter of
time before I would get a room where the big money flowed. What we
expected—and hoped for—was that I would be moved, on occasion,
into one of the traffic rooms to hear major offenses. Then I would be
in a position to market expensive favors to the various bagmen.

The big problem was that I didn't want to fix a real case. I was still
waiting for my official papers, and I was getting more uneasy by the
hour. At the same time, I felt I wouldn't be in a position to talk with, or
deal with, Judge LeFevour directly unless I was one of his top "kinks."

Ira was confident he could get me into a lucrative position. I didn't
want to turn him off, but I didn't want him to get the job done too
soon either. The fall of 1981 and the spring of 1982 seemed to be
spent in turning him on and off, depending on whether or not authorization seemed imminent. I was afraid that by the time I got authorization from the FBI to actually fix a real case, it might be too late to
strike a deal with Ira and LeFevour.

When I began this project, I thought I was going to charge in like Quantrill's Raiders and bring LeFevour to his knees in a short time. Now, after many weeks of interviews and of recording evidence, we were nowhere near ready. At the time, it all seemed like a big waste. Patience is not one of my virtues.

Perhaps because of the emotional strain—caused by my fear of discovery compounded by my frustration with the FBI—I was physically exhausted. I couldn't sleep in strange surroundings, and I was worried about how much weight I was losing. The constant stress was aging me substantially. My hair seemed suddenly to turn gray. I felt old and discouraged.

I also felt guilty about taking Jessica (then three years old) along on this adventure, but in the fall of 1981, with her mother working on a university degree, I had no alternative. Nevertheless, I felt terrible every Monday when I had to waken Jessica long before dawn so that we could catch a six o'clock plane to Chicago. On the plus side, I was able to enroll her in a top-rate day school and to hire a live-in babysitter, so she thought it was great. Kids seem to adjust to changes in surroundings more easily than adults. Yet I knew my daughter needed a stable environment and a regular routine—another reason I wanted to hasten the end of the investigation.

I was never really concerned that Ira, Tommie, or their contacts would harm my daughter. What did worry me was that if they got to me, Jessica would be left with a babysitter or at her day-care center, where a stranger would have to explain what happened to her father. That horrifying thought haunted me throughout Operation Greylord.

During this time, I got to know my daughter better and to appreciate her more. As a result, we have remained close. I found it to be a really nice break in the day (and a way to get my mind off numerous problems) to spend time as a companion to a curious, wide-eyed three-year-old.

I got to see the city from her perspective, which was interesting and frequently amusing. Most free afternoons we would walk along the lake or downtown investigating things and places and people. Jessica would ask questions, and I would try to explain. We would swim at an indoor pool, then we would go home, eat dinner, and maybe watch television with our housekeeping-babysitter.

Those quiet moments with Jessica actually kept me afloat during the project. In looking back, they are the only pleasant memories I have of the period between the summer of 1981 and the summer of 1982.

It wasn't long after I realized that Ira was a true kink, and perhaps the biggest bagman in the system, that I began to have doubts about the security of the project.

Ira obviously had tremendous clout. He could fix difficult cases. He could get major favors done by any number of powerful people. But he couldn't get me in a major room, even after all of LeFevour's regular judges, with the exception of Judge McCollom, had left the building. No one could figure out why—myself included—and it worried me. Something wasn't going right.

After Judge LeFevour had been elevated to the position of presiding judge for the First Municipal District, Judge Dan White had been put in as the head of traffic court. Everyone assumed he was just a figurehead. He was an innocuous man, probably with good intentions, who seemed to have no idea what was going on.

He would go jogging every afternoon. And then, as Ira put it, we would "steal the building."

The front office, Judge White's new domain, was still being run by the old LeFevour contingency. But something odd was going on. As the kinky judges left the building for more lucrative assignments in gun court, drug court, and theft court, they were not replaced by crooks.

Instead, the people who were put in the major rooms were all new, enthusiastic, and apparently honest individuals. Everyone assumed LeFevour was calling the shots. He appeared to be in every other way. No one could figure out why the reformation was occurring.

A possible explanation surfaced one day during an argument with Megary. I still did not have authorization to fix real cases, and I told him it was crazy for me to continue suggesting a major assignment to Ira. I might very well get trapped into having to fix something to prove my loyalty. I reminded Megary that if I did that, in addition to being unethical it was, in fact, a crime.

"Damn it, Bill," I hounded him, "don't you realize I could be prosecuted by the state's attorney for fixing a case? Doesn't anyone in the FBI know this?"

Megary assured me there was no problem because the bureau trusted Rich Daley. I told him I was insulted. He knew better than to use that explanation to mollify me. Sheepishly, he admitted that Daley had been advised of the project—at least about the traffic court aspect.

I was furious! But I thought I finally knew the reason for the clean court policy that LeFevour had adopted. The original complaint about judicial corruption had involved only traffic court—in the major rooms. As I understood it, Bernard Carey and Judge Richard Fitzgerald, who was in charge of the criminal division, had requested an investigation of what was going on in traffic court during LeFevour's reign.

If I was right, LeFevour knew traffic court was being investigated. I wondered how long it would be before my involvement became common knowledge. I could almost see my body floating down the dirty Chicago River.

More and more, I felt I was wasting my time and risking a lot for very little. Probably, in the scope of things, what I did was important. But as I waited . . . and waited . . . for authorization from the federal government and for an appointment to a major room, my enthusiasm and morale evaporated. It seemed that both my nights and days were filled with anxiety attacks—and some of these were justified.

Despite my position as a trusted confidant, I never really let down my guard with Tommie and, particularly, with Ira. Perhaps this was because Ira was so physically menacing—not that Tommie, with his .38 pistol, wasn't.

Probably the most frightening moments I spent during Operation Greylord were about five minutes in a Merchandise Mart bakery with Ira. It was in the fall of 1981—about the same time I had begun to feel uneasy about Judge White's attempts to clean up traffic court. I had asked Ira what was going on, and he had been puzzled too. Now he wanted to talk.

Ira took me to The Cookie Factory, a cheery shop gaily decorated with emerald green formica and canary yellow awnings. It was convenient to traffic court, not even a block away, and we went there on occasion for morning coffee and court gossip. I sat down in a rickety ice cream parlor chair, my back to the shop's entrance. Ira was deadly serious. His mood frightened me.

My own tremors were shaking the chair, but I tried to be casual as I asked him, "So what's going on?"

Ira looked at me, expressionless. "The deputies found a wire in the building," he said. He continued to stare at me.

I was sure he could see all of the paraphernalia I was wearing. I couldn't speak for a moment. I was ready to confess, ask for forgiveness, then run like hell. I tried to look confused, and finally I stammered, "What's a wire?"

When he explained, I heaved a sigh of relief. Thank God, he described a transmitter, not a body recorder like the one I was wearing.

Nevertheless, I thought it was all over. I couldn't imagine there being two wires in the building at the same time.

"How do you know?" I asked.

"The deputies located it on someone," he said. His eyes were cold and wary. "They're following him around right now."

I couldn't resist a quick glance over my shoulder to see if I was being tailed. My heart was pounding like a jackhammer.

"How did they locate it?" I asked.

I felt reborn when he explained. The deputies had found a transmitter while patting down a man on his way from the lockup. They hadn't let on, and let him through. The plan was to follow him to see where he went.

But now I had a new fear—less immediate and less personal, but very real. I was afraid that one of our contrived defendants might lead the deputies to Victor's office or to the bureau. But surely they wouldn't go into the lockup with a wire. That would be crazy! Then again, it wouldn't have surprised me too much.

Finally, when I had my composure back, I checked with Megary. He knew nothing about the other wire. As it turned out, this was our first encounter with the Chicago NBC affiliate's independent investigation of traffic court. Our people were not exposed, but Channel 7's investigative reporter, Peter Karl, was making our job harder—even if he didn't know about Operation Greylord.

The Chicago news media dug up exposés on traffic court at fairly regular intervals. Karl's initial efforts to mine this highly productive field turned up a few segments on the lenient treatment so common-place for major offenders charged with driving under the influence.

Apparently, after these first few segments aired on the nightly news, Karl was contacted by an irate citizen who had paid off a warrant officer to settle some parking tickets. By some oversight, the tickets had not been dismissed as promised. The citizen wanted Karl to check into this offbeat consumer fraud.

Karl's inquiry produced some hard evidence that supported the citizen's complaint. In a rather unusual procedure, the citizen had written a check, and it had indeed been cashed by one of the court's warrant officers, a man named McCauslin. In addition to endorsing the check, the warrant officer gave the citizen a piece of paper that should have gone to the clerk's office.

Neither the citizen nor Karl could make sense of the cryptic mes-sage on the paper: the letters N.S. and O.K. and a small, squiggly mark. A clerk, on the other hand, would have known that N.S. meant "non-suit"; O.K. meant the approval of someone whose approval counted and the mark was his abbreviated signature. Tommie called it his monogram. Upon receiving the message, the clerk would have dismissed the case. But through the officer's carelessness, a dissat-isfied customer and an investigative reporter had all the information they needed to bust him.

"Non-suit" is courtroom shorthand for a prosecutor's decision not to proceed with a prosecution. It is a legitimate and efficient way to prevent weak or insignificant cases from clogging the courts. Just as a policeman is allowed discretion about whether or not to write a ticket, a prosecutor has the right to decide whether or not to proceed with a case. But this scrap of paper was part of the evidence that a legitimate power was being abused in the world of traffic court.

"Monograms" aren't necessary where justifiable dismissals occur!

The scam works like this. A warrant is issued for violators with ten or more tickets. Bond is set at ten dollars per ticket. Instead of a violator being arrested, a warning letter is sent and a warrant officer visits or calls. During their conversation, the violator might ask the officer whether there is any way to avoid the twenty dollar per ticket penalty.

The warrant officer, or perhaps a precinct captain or other political functionary who is in the know, would indicate that the city might be willing to settle for half the amount, immediately and in cash. This happens to be the amount of the cash bond. The warrant officer or ward politician then takes the money to corporation counsel's office, to an attorney with "non-suit" powers. Any one of five or six attorneys could mark the warrant "N.S." and take the paper to a judge for his "O.K." and his coded signature. That scrawl would be recognized by only a few people in the clerk's office, and they would simply make the necessary entry to show that the case had been non-suited, or dismissed.

Peter Karl had found out very little about traffic court until he hit the McCauslin story. He realized he had stumbled onto more than a story about a crooked cop, but he had no idea how big the story was. What he had uncovered was the paperwork behind a fix, but he didn't know what he had. When he set out to determine if the city had gotten the irate citizen's money, everyone in traffic court stonewalled.

I wanted the U.S. attorney's office to help Karl get records by issuing some subpoenas, but everyone else seemed to think we should just lie low and wait for the publicity to blow over.

Even as Karl groped for understanding, the judicial machinery went to work on a cover-up.

Judge LeFevour was soon tipped off about Karl's operation. He called a meeting with the real powers of traffic court: Judge Mc-Collom, Judge White's assistant; the head of corporation counsel's office; and Ira.

Everyone in the building assumed that the meeting was to discuss disposing of Judge White, who was unaware the meeting had even been called. But word came out later to "flatten the building." That meant all illegal operations were to cease while Karl was snooping around.

Both Ira and Tommie were concerned, with good reason, about what might happen if Karl's investigation got out of hand. It could take LeFevour, everyone's Chinaman, down—and a flattened building was hardly a good business climate.

Despite LeFevour's best efforts, Karl stumbled onto one of LeFevour's best paying enterprises—fixing parking tickets.

In addition to his ability to non-suit cases, LeFevour had authority to grant orders of supervision, an alternative generally employed in dismissing charges against larger and more visible multiple parking offenders. If the offender was a large corporation with multiple parking violations on company vehicles, it might not look good if the cases were non-suited. In those cases, the offender would be placed on court supervision.

The only cost or fine assessed under this system was the ten dollars per ticket payoff. However, at the end of the supervision period, an order had to be entered dismissing the case. Both Tommie and Ira were concerned that LeFevour might not be willing, under the circumstances, to sign these orders on cases already bought and paid for. They were convinced the resulting publicity could bring LeFevour down. And they feared they might go down with him.

For a couple of days after Karl's story broke, Judge McCollom and the head of corporation counsel's office met behind closed doors, trying to figure out what to do.

Karl persistently called the head of corporation counsel's office, asking to see records. He was told the records were protected by privacy laws, a stand the corporation counsel's office knew to be untrue, but it bought valuable time. Court files, with only a few exceptions, are public records in this country. But Karl was not getting anywhere. He began to take steps to go to court to get the records he wanted. Apparently he was learning something about the system.

Meanwhile, Karl had managed to catch the warrant officer on camera making damaging statements. The officer protested that he hadn't kept any money; he insisted that he had given it to LeFevour.

Everyone was doing their best to stonewall—to play dumb—but the situation was getting worse. Greylord was quickly put on ice until the "Karl Caper" dissipated.

In a short time the danger had passed.

Records of the non-suited cases were taken quietly from traffic court building and stored or destroyed, according to Tommie. When their disappearance was questioned, head of corporation counsel's office explained that such records were not required to be kept, nor were they routinely kept. The paper trail that could have led Karl to the story of a lifetime was gone.

Channel 7 briefly continued to pursue the matter. The station hired one of Chicago's most prestigious law firms to go after the microfilm records stored in the circuit clerk's office. When the firm was hired, everyone in the building, Tommie and Ira included, breathed a sigh of relief.

Ira explained. "We get along good with those guys. They won't push too hard."

They were confident the case would be stalled in the courts for months—maybe years, if necessary.

Nobody could win a fight with the courts in Chicago!

However, troubles for McCauslin and the rest of the warrant officers weren't over yet. The Chicago police department's internal affairs division began to rumble about investigating all warrant officers' activities.

Rather than deal with this new problem, all the warrant officers simply resigned. They were immediately hired back by corporation counsel's office, and they were given arrest powers by the Cook County sheriff. In other words, they were now outside the jurisdiction of the police department's internal affairs division. Their salaries, benefits, and retirement all remained the same.

What a smooth, well-oiled organization. I almost had to admire it.

I was later to find that, as far as Peter Karl was concerned, the most spectacular part of his investigation was discovering the parking ticket scam.

But as far as I was concerned, the most dramatic—and frightening—development was his putting a second wire in the building. It was one of his people who was wearing the transmitter the deputies had discovered in the lockup.

Ira indicated that LeFevour would "bury" Karl for his trouble.

I later wondered if it was more than coincidence that Karl suddenly left Channel 7 and went to work for another television station!

Ira Blackwood, former Chicago police officer (copyrighted, Chicago Tribune Company, all rights reserved, used with permission)

Bernard Carey, former
State's Attorney

Terrence Hake, former Assistant
State's Attorney

Richard F. LeFevour, former Presiding Judge, First Municipal District (Wide World Photos)

Daniel Reidy, Assistant U.S. Attorney

(A) Charles Sklarsky, former Assistant U.S. Attorney

(B) Thomas P. Sullivan, former U.S. Attorney

C

(C) Daniel Webb, former U.S. Attorney

William Webster, Director, Central Intelligence Agency

Q: Were some of the provisions of this agreement
that you entered into, this additional agreement
with the federal government, reduced to writing
at some point?

A: Eventually. In the late fall of 1981, I was not
getting a major courtroom, and I didn't feel my
continued participation was that valuable. The
United States attorney's office and the FBI
wanted me to continue. I did not want to
continue. In November and December of 1981 we
entered into an agreement, an additional
agreement, which ultimately was put into
writing in January of 1982.

Q: I show you what is marked as Government's
Exhibit Lockwood No. 1, a multi-page document
dated January 6 of 1982, and ask you whether
you recognize that?

A: Yes, I do.

Q: What is it?

A: This is the letter of agreement with regard to
my continued participation in the project.

Washington Commitment

It was not quite 6:00 A.M. that cold November morning in 1981. I was
standing in a doorway behind the River Plaza apartment, just off
Rush Street. Though I stayed out of the Lake Michigan breeze, the
temperature and the tension of the morning made me shiver.

It was impossible to see the sky above the neon lights of Rush
Street. That is one thing I always found disconcerting about the city. I
always feel a little disoriented if I can't tell, early in the morning, what
the weather is going to be like. That day it would be particularly
important.

I was jittery—concerned about being airsick on the flight to Washington. I was also tense with anticipation about this hurriedly called
conference at FBI headquarters. Was I finally going to get my official
authorization to participate in Operation Greylord? I was afraid to let

myself believe it. So often before I had been disappointed. I tried to think of other things.

Rush Street was desolate. After the bars closed at two in the morning, there was no activity. The street was deserted. I was thankful that morning there were no observers in the area. Bill Megary pulled up in a no-frills government sedan. It might as well have said "property of the FBI" on the side.

I glanced up and down the block before I climbed in. Most of the courthouse regulars were still in bed and I wasn't worried about them, though the traffic court building was only three blocks away. However, the police, who were playing a bigger and bigger role in our activities, were always out. I was sure they could spot Agent Megary as easily as I had.

I didn't want anyone to get the idea I was anywhere other than where I was supposed to be—at home, sick in bed with the flu. Marie Dyson, my official girlfriend, would play another role that morning. Posing as my Aunt Mary, she would call the traffic court building to report that I was ill.

I had started a day earlier to lay the groundwork for my sick day. I complained to everyone who would listen that my throat was getting sore and that my voice kept fading out on the bench. Fortunately for the project, lying appeared to be a latent skill—and the FBI was helping me develop it. I seemed to be doing it all the time, and sometimes it frightened me. It was becoming too easy to tell lies— and make them sound convincing.

That day, no one except the U.S. attorneys assigned to Greylord and Squad 17 of the FBI knew who I was or what I was doing. Webb had arranged this flight to Washington to meet with William H. Webster, the FBI director. Webster's invitation for me to meet with him had shaken the bureau. Local agents were amazed, while the Washington corps seemed irritated or concerned. Few field agents ever meet the director. And as far as anyone knew, I was the first "snitch" to be accorded such a privilege.

My only thought was, "It's about time! They've held off much too long in getting me my official assignment paper."

We stopped at a diner down the street, and I ran in to get coffee. We drank it during the half-hour drive north to O'Hare International

Airport. Megary and I usually talked a lot, but not this morning for some reason. It was a quiet drive. We were both tense, and it showed.

Because he was so quiet, I knew Megary was worried. I wondered if he knew something he wasn't telling me. Was Webster going to stall me again? I decided to ask.

Megary shook his head. He was concerned about the way he was dressed. This trip had been arranged on such short notice that the suit he intended to wear was still at the cleaners. He didn't have the right color suit available that morning—and he was going to meet the director! I quickly learned that such things are important in the FBI.

However, I suspected that some of Megary's real concern stemmed from the upcoming meeting with Dana Caro, the Washington hotshot who had overseen the preliminary steps of Operation Greylord. A month before, Caro had been swaggering around the Chicago field office, snapping at his subordinates. I suspected that Megary dreaded a repeat performance before the director.

What I dreaded was the plane ride. I have never become accustomed to flying. While I wasn't afraid of crashing, I was afraid of getting airsick. I have a peculiar stomach.

As usual, most of my concerns about events to come that day were overlaid by fatigue. By then I was exhausted from the effort put into the project, and I really didn't care whether the meeting with Director Webster or assistant United States Attorney General Lowell Jenson came off or not. I just hoped for a relatively smooth flight.

At the airport, Megary and I parted company. "No need to take chances," Megary said.

When we boarded, I spotted him some ten rows ahead, but I never did see Dan Reidy, assistant U.S. attorney, among the 150 or so passengers sharing our early morning shuttle flight to Washington. I assumed he was somewhere on the plane because the three of us were to meet with Reidy's boss, Dan Webb, before our meeting with Webster and Jenson.

I seated myself next to a friendly man who, naturally, introduced himself. I had forgotten what my name was supposed to be, so I just introduced myself as an attorney from southern Illinois. The man commented that I was lucky I didn't have to work in Chicago's crooked court system, and he launched into an account of his experiences with judicial corruption. I was amused at the irony of the topic at that particular time. Talk about coincidence!

It had been four months since I made the commitment to be something more than a part-time informant for Operation Greylord. During that period my whole life had changed. I had moved my daughter Jessica to Chicago to be with me and had brought my aunt to the city as her babysitter. I had been trained to be an expert liar, which made me feel horribly guilty—it went against everything I had ever been taught. What was worse, it seemed to me that we had accomplished very little during those past four months.

The FBI's enthusiasm seemed to have evaporated after I moved to Chicago. Either that or—and this worried me even more—I was being kept in the dark about what was really happening. My commitment to the project was wavering again. If I didn't get official authorization this time, I would dump the whole thing. My life and my career were both on the line, and I was rapidly losing faith in the FBI's willingness to keep their promises. A lot of careers would go down the drain by the time Operation Greylord was over, and people in high places within the judicial system were not going to be happy with me. My popularity within the system in Illinois would drop faster than the 1929 stock market.

I had understood from the very beginning that my judicial career would be over, and I had accepted that. What I couldn't accept was the FBI's attitude. I wondered what awaited me in Washington. Would this meeting culminate in a written agreement with the bureau?

A few months earlier, I would have been flattered and excited about the summons. But by now, after four long months with little sleep, more tension than I had ever before faced, and few results, I wasn't very enthusiastic.

Two days before, in my apartment, Dan Reidy had orchestrated a preparation session for the Washington appointment. Reidy, like any good trial lawyer, knows that he has to be particularly careful with a hostile witness. That was the way he had acted with me.

Reidy knew that I was prepared not to like Webster. And he knew I was unhappy at the way I had been treated. He was concerned that my attitude might affect the director's decision about whether or not to proceed with the project.

I assured Reidy I was not going to blow the project. Although my enthusiasm had waned and I wanted out myself, I would do everything possible to keep the FBI interested. I desperately wanted Operation Greylord to succeed. Too much of my life had gone into it for me to see it fail. And I had paid a big price—both personally and professionally.

Megary and I landed at Washington's National Airport with three hours to kill before our meeting with Webb and Reidy. We decided to take in some of the sights, but at every place we visited, security officers insisted on checking Megary's briefcase. Each time he refused to relinquish it to a locker or allow anyone to check the contents. I told him to show his badge, but he wouldn't do that. He was afraid that it would somehow connect me with the FBI and, possibly, expose Greylord. Some people get crazy with being careful. Nothing I could say would convince Megary that we could safely act like tourists. It was going to be good when I could be plain old John Doe, citizen, again.

We stopped for a hotdog and finally met Webb and Reidy at the Department of Justice.

Webb assured us that, as far as he was concerned, there would be no problem in getting a letter of commitment. He thought it was appropriate. However, Webb was uncomfortable about my demand that he co-sign the letter because I no longer trusted FBI officials to fulfill their promises. Finally he agreed, reluctantly. He left with Reidy and Megary for a preliminary meeting with the Washington officials who had been assembling in the office of the assistant attorney general, Lowell Jenson.

In about thirty minutes, Megary returned, all smiles now. He told me everything was going well, and it was time to meet with the rest of the participants.

I joined Webb and Reidy who were in Jenson's outer office. With them were Lowell Jenson, Dana Caro, Gerald McDowell from the department of Public Integrity section (he had been my original contact with Greylord), and FBI director William Webster.

We moved into Jenson's inner office and arranged ourselves around a coffee table. The room was full of museum-quality antiques. Ironically, I was seated on a loveseat next to Dana Caro.

Webster was seated to my right, and Jenson was across the coffee table from me.

Much to my surprise, as the meeting progressed, I was favorably impressed by Webster. Reidy had predicted that I would finally come to like the man. It looked as if his prediction was right.

A quiet man, Webster was rather reserved and thoughtful—almost shy. He had none of the politician's mannerisms that I had expected. Instead, he looked as if he might be more comfortable in an academic setting.

Webster had been a federal judge in St. Louis, Missouri, before Jimmy Carter appointed him director of the FBI in 1978. I knew very little about him and would certainly not have recognized him from previous publicity. I had been led to believe that he was a rather dictatorial character. A few weeks earlier, Bob Walsh, Dana Caro's assistant in Washington, told Megary that the director had frowned at some aspects of the case. Everyone had gone crazy trying to interpret that expression.

Webster's concerns about Greylord were not at all political. He was concerned about many of the same things that bothered me throughout the project. There are ethical, moral, and legal problems in investigating judges in the first place. Furthermore, it was difficult to figure out just how to conduct such an investigation appropriately. Webster impressed me as having a good understanding of these complications, both theoretical and practical. I felt somewhat reassured.

Webster listened attentively throughout our session. Jenson was more energetic, making points forcefully. I was relieved to find that both men seemed knowledgeable and aware of the progress and pitfalls of the Greylord operation. I also came away feeling confident that neither of these individuals was afraid to take on the project. That was very important to me.

However, we all knew that Operation Greylord was a political hot potato! Congress had been furious about Abscam. Everyone understood that if the opportunity arose to chastise the justice department or the FBI about witch hunts, Congress would certainly grab the chance. If we were not effective in handling the problems in Chicago, we would all be in a lot of trouble.

Webster voiced his concern that the criminal elements came to me to talk about their activities. He was afraid I might be doing something to coerce otherwise innocent people into engaging in criminal conduct. In other words, like everyone else, he was afraid of entrapment. A judge, because of his position of power and influence, could easily pressure innocent people into violating the law.

However, I think I put his fears to rest in this regard. "Judge Webster," I began, "I know it's hard to understand a judicial system that is essentially political—not judicial."

Webster interrupted, "I don't understand what you mean by that."

I replied, "I think everything gets distorted when the politicians decide to put a candidate on the ballot. If you get put on the ballot in a one-party system like Chicago's, you're elected. So the slatemakers decide who is going to be a judge. They want to reward people who have been loyal in the past and who are going to be loyal in the future—mostly hacks."

"That sounds really depressing," Webster commented.

"It is depressing," I answered. "And it means that most of the people on the bench are viewed as lackeys by the politicians and the public. There seems to be no respect for judges unless they have a lot of political pull someplace. Most of these people are at the bottom of the system. Everybody looks down at them—everybody talks down to them."

I continued. "The crooks work for the bagmen. Once a bagman encourages or seduces some judge into taking money, he might as well own that judge.

"These guys look at me as a judge they can potentially market. They are not threatened by me because they are used to having judges who work for the politicians. Probably I am less a threat to them than their own judges because I'm an outsider. They know I've got no clout and that no one would pay attention to me if I turned on them."

I went on. "You've heard the tape where Tommie's bragging about how many whores he's made of judges. From what I've seen, that's a pretty good description."

Webster and Jenson sat quietly for a moment, contemplating what I had said. I wondered if they found the system as frightening as I did. Finally Jenson began to speak. He told me how much both he and

Director Webster appreciated my assistance in the project. They both expressed their strong support for Greylord in general and for me in particular. They assured me I would have my official letter of authorization in January.

I breathed a sigh of relief. At last I had a firm commitment—a specific date when I would receive my official papers.

And this time, after meeting Director Webster in person, I felt sure I was finally on safe ground. He had been very convincing.

BLACKWOOD: I mean you don't just talk to anybody. You have to know who the thing comes from. You know what I mean? That's like you got some guy that knows everything, you keep it down to a restricted few, you know. Anyhow, all you gotta do is just do your job, that's all. The only thing they want to do is know where they're goin' with their guy, that's all. Nobody said that you have to send them to jail . . . some cases you have to. You know. But they want, instead of nine months ya give 'em three months, or whatever the case. You know what I mean?

JUDGE LOCKWOOD: Yeah.

BLACKWOOD: That could be a freebie. Cause if they go in there, they don't know where they're goin'. That's the big complaint.

JUDGE LOCKWOOD: (Sighs)

BLACKWOOD: That's the whole thing in a nutshell.

12

1313 Ritchie Court

I had "re-upped" for another six-month tour of duty in Chicago after meeting with FBI director William Webster in Washington during November, 1981. I was confident I had made the right decision, especially when I reported on January 16, 1982, for my first work assignment of the new year.

Jack Thorpe, my FBI contact, met me at Meigs Field with the protection I had been promised in Washington—a letter authorizing me to accept payoffs, if necessary "to affect the outcome of appropriate cases that come before you as a sitting judge."

Thorpe displayed the letter like a historical document—which I guess in some ways it was. The letter also authorized me to talk to other judges, attorneys, and bagmen regarding cases arranged by the FBI.

This was the insurance policy I had been after for months. Now it was finally down in black-and-white under the signatures of

125

FBI special agents-in-charge James O. Ingram and Dan Webb. I didn't know who Ingram was, but Webb was a man I felt I could trust.

My relief was tempered by uneasiness. A sentence in the second paragraph set my nerves on edge. Ingram and Webb had obtained the authorization in consultation with the state's attorney (Richard M. Daley) and the chief judge of the criminal court of Cook County (Richard Fitzgerald).

I knew nothing about Fitzgerald, good or bad, but at least I knew of nothing to connect him with LeFevour. My exasperation with the agency's reckless trust of Daley returned full force.

Thorpe hastened to reassure me. "They don't know your name," he said. "They only know we've got a downstate judge involved."

"That just means guys like you wouldn't know my name," I snapped back, angry now. "There's only one downstate judge who has access to the kind of information I have. It wouldn't take Gino Superchi a minute to figure out that I'm that downstate judge."

I also doubted that Daley and Fitzgerald were really ignorant of my name. Megary had told me the previous November that Daley knew only that they had an informant working with them. Now Thorpe was telling me Daley knew their informant was a judge, and from downstate at that.

A little later, the assistant U.S. attorney tried to placate me by explaining that Fitzgerald had been involved with Greylord from the start. Another two years passed before I learned that Fitzgerald, along with Daley's Republican predecessor, Bernard Carey, had approached U.S. Attorney Tom Sullivan in 1979 about investigating corruption in the judicial system.

Megary also assured me later that I had nothing to fear from Fitzgerald. I accepted his assurance about Fitzgerald, but I never felt comfortable about Daley.

After our discussion of the letter, Thorpe and I turned the conversation to what should have been a noncombustible topic—my living arrangements for the next few months. I mentioned that Kathy, my girlfriend from Marion, was coming the following week to help me enroll Jessica in a new day-care center and get our winter schedule arranged.

Thorpe interjected with exactly the wrong words. "Don't tell her anything about what you're doing."

I was in no mood to hear his lecture about security when I had just discovered that two more people knew about my Greylord involvement.

"You people go around telling anybody you feel like about me and my involvement," I said, mad as hell. "Now let me tell you—I'll damn well tell people I can trust!"

When I informed him that I had already told Kathy, one police officer, and the judges from my county about my involvement, Thorpe looked shocked.

I wanted him and the rest of the FBI to know that if they messed up and I suffered as a result of their actions, people were going to ask questions. I was always fearful that if the project went bad, the bureau would try to remove itself from any responsibility. I had to make sure they were aware that other people knew of our connection.

Thorpe wouldn't concede the point. "You can't go telling people without prior approval," he insisted. "I don't even tell my wife what I'm doing at the office."

The obvious implication, of course, was that I had no right to share my secrets with a girlfriend.

"No," I shot back. "You just told Rich Daley."

We glared angrily at each other. Finally, I suggested that the agency terminate me if it didn't think I was handling my end. I left his car and stomped off toward the traffic court building.

"Well, Brock," I thought to myself, "that ends your involvement with Operation Greylord."

A month later, I was still working, and despite my impatience with their methods, I had to confess Megary and the FBI were treating me well. As Ira would have said, I had found a sponsor.

The letter over Ingram's and Webb's signatures guaranteed significant financial protection should my Greylord involvement backfire on my judicial career. It promised if I could no longer function effectively as an associate judge and faced a loss of income, the FBI would pay the equivalent of my judicial salary for a period not to exceed four months. I was fairly certain I would need that provision before much longer. I was feeling the heat from several areas.

Of immediate interest was language in the letter that not only acknowledged my "professional and personal sacrifices," but pledged the FBI to pay for all fully documented expenses directly related to my participation in the investigation.

Mostly for security reasons, the FBI decided to rent an apartment for Jessica and me. The idea was that I should be situated in a place that was, perhaps, a little too lavish for my station in life—the kind of apartment a crooked judge with ill-gotten gains might rent. Washington authorized a "suitably priced apartment," with rent and utilities not to exceed $1,272 monthly. I was to apply my $800 monthly housing allowance as a visiting judge toward the expense, and I would be reimbursed for the balance.

Thorpe and I went door-to-door looking for an apartment on the plush Gold Coast, just off Lakeshore Drive. This enclave of stately townhouses is ringed by towering highrises. It is perhaps one of the most fashionable areas in the city—convenient to downtown and only three blocks north of Rush Street. Most everyone in the neighborhood drove a Mercedes, a Volvo, or a BMW. You could even see a Rolls-Royce now and then.

We ultimately selected a two-bedroom, two-bath apartment at 1313 Ritchie Court. The apartment had a view of Lake Michigan. Although the neighborhood appeared to be safe, we were guarded from intrusions by a barrier of security that included a doorman and an automatic door-locking system.

While most of the neighborhood seemed to be inhabited by young professionals, there were some concessions made to family life. Just across the street was a well-equipped playground and park where my daughter and I played together many afternoons. Megary and I also had frequent meetings there.

On the first floor of our building was a Stop-N-Shop—a grocery store-delicatessen that catered to extremely expensive tastes. Although I enjoyed looking at all the unusual and pricey items on display, since I was cooking primarily for a three-year-old, my purchases seldom included the exotic items that were available.

I brought sufficient things from home to furnish the kitchen, and Thorpe found a confiscated television set somewhere. Jessica gave him a big hug and kiss when he brought it—much to Thorpe's embarrassment. The picture tended to fade in and out, but it was good enough for Jessica to watch Bozo the Clown at 7:00 A.M. and for me to catch Bill Kurtis on the evening news.

We rented some furniture, but it hardly began to fill the spacious living room and dining area. There weren't enough lamps, and the absence of drapes and pictures on the walls sometimes made the apartment seem gloomy. I always felt cold and desolate looking out over Lake Michigan.

Maintaining an apartment in a high-rent district presupposed that I was fixing cases. But both Ira and Tommie knew I was making very little money—a total of $100 in my first four-month stint as a crook. So I had to come up with an excuse to allay their curiosity about my wealth.

One cold January day, something plausible hit me out of the blue.

"I came on to a great deal," I told Ira and Tommie. "I'm subletting a condo for whatever the state pays me. The thing is furnished and everything. Of course, I have to let them show it whenever they want, but, what the hell? You can't beat the price, and it's a great location."

They recognized the address and were properly impressed.

"Oh, yeah," Ira remembered, "Judge Cropton* lived right across the street. He got caught on a conflict-of-interest beef—stole a ton of money, and here this conflict thing came up. He had an interest in Wells Fargo or some shit and didn't disclose it in a case he heard. The other side found out about it, and he decided to resign."

Ira paused. "He was a hell of a guy," he reflected, almost wistfully. "Broads, booze, you name it—some hellacious parties."

That convinced me Thorpe had done his legwork well. Ritchie Court was a good neighborhood for an aspiring crooked judge.

I never got over my amazement at—nor my disgust with—judges on the take. Those with extra money flaunted it. They seemed to ignore the possibility that they might have to account for the manner in which they lived. There was no way most of them could afford a Gold Coast lifestyle on a $60,000-a-year salary. Judges are barred from generating outside income, other than from traditional investments.

*Pseudonym.

I was using a car the FBI had given me that spring. It was a fairly nice-looking 1980 Pontiac that the government had confiscated in the East. But it was a piece of junk. I suspected the car had been used to run moonshine over unpaved mountain roads. Everything rattled and the motor was near exhaustion. It was hard to start and had a way of dying at intersections.

One subzero morning, Old Glory, as Jessica and I christened the car, refused to start. Cabs were almost impossible to find during bad weather, so we ended up walking the mile and a half to the daycare center. I carried Jessica under my coat. The bitter forty-mile-an-hour wind brought tears to my eyes, and as they fell, they froze on my face.

The FBI hoped the car might provide a good setting for interesting conversations, and they pushed through the paperwork necessary to wire it for sound. But, looking back, the car was probably an unnecessary expense. Not only did I have to spend several minutes every day finding a parking place downtown, the FBI had to pay an extra $100 a month for parking near the apartment.

I couldn't complain. The government was taking good care of me. It lived up to its promise to cover any expenses I incurred as a result of my extended stay in Chicago: $13 a day for the care and feeding of my horses, $30 a week for security checks at the farm, and $250 to have somebody seed and disk my ten acres of land. I was also allowed $50 a week, maximum, for transportation and $150 a week for "reciprocal entertainment expenses." It was a generous figure by FBI standards, but hardly enough to keep pace with Tommie and Ira.

One day in January, 1982, I was approached at work by Lynn Emmerman of the *Chicago Tribune*. Ms. Emmerman wanted some interesting anecdotes about traffic court. I stalled her briefly and went to talk to Judge White in the front office. I thought I could use this as an entree to develop a better relationship with him. I was still looking for an assignment to a major room.

It seemed to work, initially. White wanted me to talk to her and find out what she was looking for.

It wasn't clear whether Ms. Emmerman was more interested in uncovering inefficiency in the traffic court or in establishing her superiority over a "hillbilly" judge, but I decided to play along with her stereotype of the ignorant country judge. I told her I really didn't know anything about inefficiency in the building and was just amazed at how many people there were in the court system. When she asked if I had any trouble getting around the city, I replied that I had been off the farm twice before, so I really didn't have a problem. In answer to her question about whether I liked the Chicago people, I told her that I did.

She also wanted to know if I thought it was "ironic" that most of the people who came before me were from the ghetto. What she meant was black. I told her that wasn't ironic; there were a lot of poor people in the southern end of the state, too. I tried to seem pleasant and ignorant.

Ms. Emmerman's article came out prior to March 1, when I returned to Chicago. The gist of it was that there was a lot of corruption and other misconduct going on in the building. When I heard that LeFevour was furious, I decided I had better talk to him.

I called Squad 17 to see if LeFevour's office had been checked for metal detectors. This was supposed to have been accomplished several weeks before but as I suspected, it had not been done. I walked in that morning expecting alarms to go off. Fortunately, the office was clear. I got out of the problem with the *Tribune* by simply telling LeFevour that White had put me up to it.

But LeFevour made it clear that he still didn't like me. The feeling was mutual.

My own role in the investigation had changed significantly since the meeting with Webster in Washington, D.C., in November. Ira continued his efforts to get me into a major courtroom, and I urged him to expend more effort in that direction. I no longer had much hope for success, but it still was our best shot at getting close to LeFevour.

"We're going to find out something, today," Ira promised in early February. "We have to get going on you."

"Yeah," I agreed heartily. "But I'm still convinced you're not going to get me assigned to a good room without me putting up some money."

"If there's any rent involved, we'll know about it," Ira assured me. "The only rent you have to pay is when they call and say, 'Hey, take care of this one,' and that's it."

"That's it," echoed Tommie, pushing in on the conversation. He was trying to keep a hand in the action.

"You take care of it, and there's no coupons," Ira said, ignoring him. "You know what I mean? It's free-ola for you."

But despite Ira's assurances and intervention, it became increasingly clear that the presiding judge, Dan White, planned to keep straight people in the major rooms.

Ira was really pushing for me now, trying to find openings. He finally saw an opportunity in mid-March. It looked as if Judge Howard Kaufman might be out a few weeks for an operation, and Ira wanted me to talk to Judge White right away.

"We gotta break down the damn barrier," he kept saying. "Once we get past there, then we'll be in—periodically, anyway."

Ira had big plans for me. Business in the building had been bad lately. None of the judges in the major rooms seemed interested in any action, and lots of hustlers, Tommie included, were feeling the pinch of lean times.

"When you get in there, we'll get rid of four or five cases in one day . . . that's all," Ira promised. "And don't worry. You ain't gonna be doin' nothing that anybody else doesn't do."

I talked to Judge White. As I had suspected, he wasn't interested. He was cordial, but he said he wanted to keep Chicago judges in the major courtrooms. For once, Ira's backing was a detriment. White wanted judges he could trust in his rooms, and having Ira back me didn't exactly inspire White's trust.

Traffic court had changed since the days LeFevour ruled as presiding judge. Shortly after LeFevour left to become presiding judge of the First Municipal District, in January, 1981, he began to reassign his judges within his expanded domain. None of the replacements White named in traffic court seemed to be on the take. It was a marked departure from LeFevour's taste in subordinates. The new judges all seemed squeaky clean and interested in getting the job done.

Ira had been in a dither since October, wondering what was going on. Judge Harry Branson* seemed to be the only judge in a major room who might be kinky.

---

*Pseudonym.

White's sudden interest in housecleaning made me uneasy—I sensed that something was not right. That feeling increased as spring approached. White seemed a competent enough judge, but he was no reformer. Was it possible that he was still nervous about Peter Karl's investigation of the preceding October? Karl had never really known how close to the bone he cut, so I couldn't convince myself that a watchful press was the sole motivation behind White's tactics. There had to be more to it.

Ira and Tommie were uneasy, too. Business had tapered off considerably, and Tommie's high-flying life style was hurting. But he was an optimist.

"I got that feeling in my fucking bones it's gonna pick up soon," he sighed in early February.

Ira countered boastfully. "Things are good for me. I have no complaints. I'm in good shape. Did very well."

"Yeah," Tommie said, "but not on the building."

"No, not on the building," Ira agreed. "No, but. . . ."

"No, hey, on side things," Tommie reminded him.

"Yeah," Ira said, after a moment. "The building ain't doin' all right."

LeFevour had gotten into the habit of making sudden, unannounced appearances in the traffic court building or in White's office. We all wondered a lot about these impromptu visits. Word was that they always left White looking like a whipped pup. Many building regulars, Ira included, believed that White was not really in charge of the traffic court building. Ira regarded White as little more than a mouthpiece for LeFevour. In fact, White hadn't even been consulted when the real powers of traffic court plotted to stop Karl's investigation cold.

One other question remained unanswered. Why didn't White put anyone in the major rooms who could do LeFevour some good? It didn't fit.

I had a theory that explained all the odd goings-on, but I hoped like hell I was wrong. The traffic court building's bad business climate, White's clean appointees, and LeFevour's police tactics all seemed to indicate that the Chief knew someone was looking at the traffic court building.

I had seen and heard enough about Judge White to know he wasn't the kind of man who could stand up to a powerhouse like Richard LeFevour. He was an honest man; a gentleman—not a street fighter. If LeFevour really wanted to put somebody in traffic court to make some money, White wouldn't be able to stop him. As a result, I had to conclude that LeFevour didn't want anyone dishonest in those rooms right now.

Ira complained constantly that prosecutors from Daley's office wouldn't cooperate on anything—especially drunken driving charges. Daley's staff handled the prosecutions in the major rooms, and it was the major rooms that were being made snow white. Under "orders from Rich," prosecutors were to recommend jail time or heavy fines on every case, or face losing their jobs. In effect, a judge who wanted to take a draw had to do it on his own, because Daley's people steered clear of any hint of leniency.

By spring, I was firmly convinced that LeFevour had cleaned up his act because of our investigation.

It began to seem as if I were playing some kind of game—a game in which the level of difficulty increased each time I performed a task successfully. I had finally made my way through the maze of bureaucracy, and although I hadn't scored many points, I had passed through relatively unscathed. Then, I had scored a few points on the streets, escaping the detection that would have brought the game to a sudden and undesirable end. Now I found myself dodging other pitfalls.

Squad 17's latest moves didn't add to my sense of security. In response to my pleadings, Dan Reidy and Chuck Sklarsky, another assistant U.S. attorney, finally agreed to work on getting a warrant to tap Ira's phone. Entrusted with a few odd jobs to help out, I confirmed the number on Ira's telephone by taking a call there from my FBI girlfriend, Marie Dyson.

It took about sixty days to get the taps authorized and installed on Ira's phone. Numerous security safeguards were used to ensure that no one knew a federal wiretap was in place. In most places, I'm sure these procedures would have been adequate, but not in Chicago.

Almost immediately after the wiretap went into effect, Ira stopped using his telephone. Megary and the others didn't believe there was a problem, but I knew that we had blown it, somehow. My suspicions

were confirmed a few days later when Carl, an assistant in corporation counsel's office, grabbed my arm in a hallway.

"Hey, watch what you say on the phone these days," he warned.

My heart almost stopped. "What do you mean?"

"The boss has a friend at Illinois Bell who says three lines in the
building are tapped—legally." Carl glanced up and down the hallway,
as if a ghost was spying on him. Just thought you might like to know.
Don't go calling anybody's wife for a date." He grinned.

I tried to laugh naturally. "I'm keeping clean. Who are they really
after?"

"We don't know yet, but we're working on it," he assured me.
"Probably White, my office, maybe the clerk's office. We'll know for
sure by the end of the day."

I walked away thanking him—and cursing the lax security.

Once again, LeFevour's organization seemed to be demonstrating
its superiority over the FBI. I tried to prepare myself. I believed it was
just a matter of time—probably a short time—before they were wise
to me.

I made a panicky call to Megary, who called the U.S. attorney's
office. Sklarsky decided he had better meet me after work, to calm me
down. He assured me that Carl's information wasn't nearly as good
as Carl thought it was. Four lines had been tapped, not three. But
despite Sklarsky's assurances, I knew we had wasted a couple of
months getting those taps.

More and more things were spooking me. Victor and I returned to
traffic court together after lunch a couple of days later, and we spent
another few minutes talking outside corporation counsel's office. I
noticed Carl walk past as we were talking. He was waiting for me as I
walked toward my courtroom.

"What are you doing talking to that guy?" he demanded.

I was taken aback at his tone, but managed to keep cool. "He used
to be one of my students at Southern Illinois University," I said.
"What's the problem?"

"We think he's the 'G*,' " Carl growled, watching my reaction.

I didn't have any trouble looking panicked. No doubt the recorder

*G-man, or federal agent.

picked up the pounding of my heart. "If that's right, I'm in trouble," I groaned. I prayed Carl had no idea of the extent of the "trouble."

"You just better stay away from him," Carl replied.

I tried to get him to explain why they thought Victor worked for the government, but Carl only repeated his warning to steer clear.

It made me uncomfortable that the bad guys knew about me and my personal life, but there was no way around it. I misled them from time to time, but I had to be careful not to stray too far from the truth. Friends, other judges, and other attorneys might easily contradict my statements, and I could not afford to lose credibility.

Again I felt the strain of constantly being on guard. Things seemed to happen continually to test my control. After one long evening of drinking, Ira insisted on coming to my apartment to use the bathroom. I was still sober enough to realize I had left several tapes and transcripts on a living room table. With my pulse easily topping one hundred, I steered Ira straight to the bathroom, then quickly scooped up everything on the table and stuffed it into a kitchen cabinet.

On another occasion, Ira insisted on taking me to try on coats at Merchandise Mart. It was an effort, but I managed to resist the salesman's efforts to assist me in donning the coats. On yet another occasion, Ira wanted me to join him in a steam bath. I suddenly had a date with Marie!

I don't believe such incidents would have been as nerve-racking had I assumed a different identity during my days with Greylord. I wasn't really undercover, as the term is generally understood. I was being myself—Brocton Lockwood, a trial judge from downstate Illinois—and that was who I wanted to go on being. If I couldn't be a judge, I wanted to be an attorney again. And to retain my license to practice law, I had to retain my own identity.

Of course, I had no guarantee I would be able to practice law after I was through with Greylord—or it was through with me—especially if I ever fixed a real case.

"My God!" I exclaimed to myself. "Whatever in kingdom come possessed me to push myself into this mess? I must have been insane."

Q: Did you determine from your examination of those documents what the charges were that were pending against David Washington in those complaints?

A: Yes

Q: What were those charges?

A: He was convicted in 1975 with driving while suspended or revoked. He was placed on probation for that. He did not comply with the terms of probation. He was then charged in 1978 and 1980 with driving under the influence and driving while suspended or revoked and some minor charges. He was also charged in 1979 with driving while suspended and a minor charge. I think he had a wreck. At the time of the last entry, he had four driving-while-suspended, two driving under the influence, and about four minor moving violations.

13

Caught with Pants Down

By the spring of 1982, my role had changed. It was obvious that I was not going to be able to deal directly with LeFevour. Not only did we dislike one another, but he was too well insulated by his bagmen and crooked judges.

LeFevour's underlings, however, *were* vulnerable. His bagmen and corrupt judges became the immediate targets. So, rather than try to deal directly with LeFevour, my primary task was to identify his crooked associates and determine the nature of the cases to be presented.

I didn't believe Gino Superchi or Ira would voluntarily cooperate, regardless of the amount of pressure that was put on them. But I wasn't quite so sure about Judge LeFevour's other major bagmen— his cousin Jimmy, for example. Jimmy had a lot of personal problems, he had health problems, and he had a substantial drinking problem.

Judge Arthur Brandley* also had a drinking problem, and he was getting extremely sloppy. On one occasion, I saw him accept money from Ira in the hallway, in front of numerous spectators. After the David Washington case, I viewed Brandley as perhaps the most likely person to turn or flip if or when a case was made against him. The man seemed to be falling to pieces. And with what he knew, I thought he might give us Richard LeFevour on a silver plate.

The David Washington case became our first chance to try out our new tactics. Washington had paid money to keep from going to jail. But when he and his attorney, Brad Jenkins*, appeared in court on February 3, 1982, Judge Brandley sentenced Washington to 364 days in the county jail. That was unheard of.

Attorney Jenkins' sponsor was the former county chairman, George Dunne. (I'm not suggesting that Dunne knew his name was being marketed.) That association, in and of itself, should have been enough to avoid a prison sentence. But in addition, payment had been made that should have guaranteed leniency.

"Our jaws are hitting our ankles," Jenkins told us a couple of days afterwards. "I'm doing a Jackie Gleason number—I'm a–I'm a–I'm a. . . ."

Ira was laughing despite some professional embarrassment. He was the one who had arranged with Brandley to fix Jenkins' case.

"Did your guy go to jail?" I asked. I had never heard of anybody going to jail in traffic court before, especially someone with a lawyer.

"Yeah, they grabbed him." Jenkins was laughing now, too. I couldn't understand why. "That was it. He was gone. He's been out at Cook County eating [Sheriff] Elrod's bologna sandwiches for six days now."

Washington was a six-time loser. He had piled up two drunken driving tickets and four driving after revocation tickets in the past eight years, so it was difficult to feel sorry for him. However, he had paid Brandley's price for probation, and now he was eating cold cuts.

Ira recounted what had happened. "I told Brandley about it the day before, and he said he would take care of it tomorrow. Then I got a headache that was killing me. I didn't get out of bed the whole day. So

*Pseudonym.

I thought to myself, 'Oh, Brandley will remember.' But it was after lunch—that was the problem. It was after lunch."

I chuckled knowingly in response to Ira's reference to Judge Brandley's liquid lunches.

"Yeah, his memory is clouded more than a little bit after lunch." Jenkins was still laughing.

Had I been in his place, I wouldn't have considered it so funny.

"Well, then, after it's all over with, Jenkins calls me and says, 'He got a year!' " Ira exclaimed. "So, I go see Brandley and I tell him about it. And he says, 'You know, I thought that name rang a bell. Brad Jenkins—the guy kept saying his name. He said it a dozen times or so.' "

Jenkins interjected. "You know, like, Hey it's me, Judge! Remember me?"

Ira picked up the conversation again. "Brandley took a ton of money on the thing." He shook his head. "He took the next package, too."

I wasn't sure I had heard this quite right. "He'd already been paid once, and he got paid again to fix it—but he screwed up?" I asked.

Ira nodded.

"Well that asshole," I said. "I'd thump his head for that. I'd say, 'Listen, you son of a bitch, when you get bought, you stay bought.' "

Ira laughed. "Brandley says, 'Oh, fuck, Ira. I forgot. I don't know what the hell we're going to do.' I told him, 'Damn it, Judge . . . undo it.' " Ira roared until tears came to his eyes.

Brandley followed Ira's order. He "undid it." Washington never served anything more than six days in jail.

The fact that Brandley was unable to remember when he had been bought made me think he might be LeFevour's weakest link. Squad 17 agreed. My contacts in the bureau had been working on contrived cases since our meeting with Webster. They were "choreographing" crimes designed to be marketed by LeFevour's closest judges and bagmen.

The strategy was to catch LeFevour's associates in the act of fixing cases. Then, once they were caught, the U.S. attorney's office would offer them leniency for any cooperation they might give in prosecuting those higher up the ladder.

While there were many indications that judges were fixing major cases in divorce court, housing court, and major criminal court, we had no way of obtaining cases that could be presented. Webster had drawn the line at having our targets fix real cases. He was convinced that the whole project would backfire. Critics could claim that agents had interfered with outcomes of state cases. That decision meant we had to spend a substantial amount of time creating cases to be marketed. In addition, we could use only cases that could be manufactured by agents pretending to be crooks.

Later, we would be criticized for using contrived cases. Some critics would say that our strategy of manufacturing cases had overcrowded the state court docket and perpetrated a fraud upon the court. Others would suggest that the kind of cases used in the Greylord investigation showed that only penny-ante corruption had occurred within the system.

Many Chicagoans shrugged their shoulders. It was no big deal. A judge fixed a drunk driver's case. So what? A precinct captain or a police officer could do the same thing.

Because there was no way agents could act out a major felony—corroborating evidence had to be obtained—Greylord was limited to fixing the kind of crimes that could cause no serious or permanent damage. Imagine the public outcry if agents had been involved in torching buildings or committing murder or rape. It is very difficult to fake any of these outcomes—they required a destroyed building, a dead body, or a violated victim. As a result, most charges fell under the label of a Class IV felony or below. This classification included minor thefts, shoplifting, gun violations, possession of narcotics, and the like.

The FBI's big fear in any sting operation is to be accused of entrapment. It was particularly important in a case as sensitive as judicial corruption to make sure that only judges who had a so-called predilection to fix cases were approached. We did not want to influence a judge to perform actions that he would not otherwise do. I functioned as an advance scout to find judges with this predilection for corruption.

The way I scouted the territory was to drink gallons and gallons of coffee. I drank coffee with almost anyone in the whole damned traffic court building! I made regular rounds in the morning, stopping to shoot the breeze with clerks, attorneys, policemen, or anyone else who might have information. I downed so much fresh-perked coffee at New Mayor's Row that the waitresses called me Mr. Coffee.

Obviously, not everyone I talked to was a target, and I tried to limit my taping of conversations to those persons who were directly involved. I picked up a great deal of interesting information in my wanderings, and I obtained enough hard leads on bonafide kinks to make up for the damage to my gastrointestinal system.

I passed this information on to Thorpe, who transferred it to Megary at FBI headquarters. The FBI and the U.S. attorney's office identified the target. Then, in conjunction with the Chicago police department's Internal Affairs Division, they would determine the kind of crime that must be created in order to present it to a targeted judge. Each scenario had to be tailor-made to fit a particular judge's specifications.

With all this background information at its disposal, Squad 17 then recruited FBI agents from throughout the United States to come to Chicago to be arrested. False identities had to be created for each defendant. I had assumed that the FBI had the capability to manufacture a new identity for an agent. But it wasn't that simple. False information had to be given to various state authorities to create a fictitious background that could stand up under a police check. A participating agent had to have pictures and other documents to obtain a current driver's license with a false identification. With this, he would obtain credit cards and other authentic trappings that could be carried in a wallet.

The level of professionalism during the planning stages was above criticism. But trouble began when agents took their scenarios into the field and tried to get arrested. It was a problem to find agents who could take themselves out of character long enough to look and act like criminals.

It would have been easy for drug enforcement agents to get themselves arrested. Because of their training, they could look like ragedy-ass street people—bleary-eyed, smelly, the whole thing. But FBI agents, for some reason, didn't seem to be able to project themselves that way. They acted like honest, straightforward people, and their appearance worked against them. Most of the agents were white and clean-cut. They just didn't look suspicious.

One blonde agent with a pleasant face tried again and again to get arrested for shoplifting. He couldn't pull it off despite bagging several hundred dollars worth of merchandise. I had no idea it was so difficult to get arrested.

Finally, the scenario was altered to include a complaining witness who reported the offender to the store management. We began to use a second witness in almost every case. That way we could be sure the complaining witness would show up in court to testify, in the event the police failed to be present.

Another way to proceed against the primary targets was by using phone taps. Then cases wouldn't have to be created, or outcomes of real cases wouldn't have to be altered. However, before the very drastic step of tapping someone's phone can be taken, probable cause must be established to the satisfaction of a magistrate. For several months, I had asked the FBI to try to establish probable cause to tap both Ira's and Bert Pillar's phones. They both used the phone to contact judges and/or clients on a regular basis. I was sure we could obtain a substantial amount of information.

Because the FBI ignored my requests, I finally went directly to the U.S. attorney's office. Sklarsky was more receptive to the idea.

We decided to tap Ira's line again. He seemed to be the best target. Maybe we'd have better luck this time. Victor and I searched our field notes and memories for evidence to show that Ira used his phone in connection with various cases that had been fixed. While we were gathering this information, and Marie Dyson was attempting to get authorization out of Washington to present it to a magistrate, everyone else worked on contrived cases.

After the first of the year, I didn't do quite as much socializing with the bad guys as I had earlier. As the project went on, I avoided more and more social contact with the targets and their families. It was just too emotionally devastating, and it hadn't really proved to be very productive. I seemed to discover a lot more in the daytime than I did at night.

On one occasion, however, Marie and I went to dinner at Tommie's place. Tommie envisioned himself as a gourmet cook—and he was very good. It was an excellent meal.

Ira was there, along with Tommie's date and Tommie's father. The elder Kangalos was a pleasant old Greek immigrant who appeared to have been an honest, hardworking man all of his life. He was obviously disturbed about his high-living youngest child. And I was upset when I thought about the pain we were going to bring the old man, through his son. I hated to abuse Tommie's hospitality, but I rationalized that it was just part of the job.

On March 29, I returned to Chicago from a weekend at home, discouraged and exhausted. I had reached the point where I couldn't shake the tension, even in southern Illinois. I had bad dreams almost every night, and I usually awoke around 3:00 A.M., unable to go back to sleep.

Agent Thorpe met me with news that one of the contrived cases had blown up over the weekend. He explained that two agents had come in from out of town to play the roles of a defendant and a complaining witness. They had been supplied with phoney identifications.

Unfortunately, one of the agents, the defendant, failed to leave his real FBI identification behind when he and his partner went to Water Tower Place to stage the attempted theft of the partner's wallet. When the agent/defendant was arrested, the police found his real identification, as well as the false identification. They searched his partner, the complaining witness, and found he was wearing a body recorder. Both men were quickly identified as FBI agents, and the story hit the press.

I was sick and angry.

The police apparently thought they had uncovered an investigation of police misconduct. Although I was relieved about that, instinctively I knew we had problems. Our cover had been blown. Everyone would be suspicious now.

When I got to the traffic court building and talked to Ira and Tommie, I discovered no real harm had been done. As soon as I got a break, I called Squad 17 to tell them everything in the building was okay. Everyone there thought it was an investigation of the police department, too. Nobody knew what was really going on!

I asked Thorpe not to let the bureau or the U.S. attorney's office ditch all our cases. I was sure that would be going through their minds. But he informed me that the decision had already been made.

All of the contrived cases now in the works would be scrapped. They would not begin to contrive any new cases for six weeks.

A couple of hours later I called Sklarsky and told him I would be quitting in thirty days.

KANGALOS: I, ah, I (garbled) I don't relate
to . . . Dick (LeFevour), I don't have to.

> BLACKWOOD: He, ah, yeah, he used to make an
> enemy out of everyone, you know, he's got, he's
> got them, ah, vacuum cleaner pockets. (Laughs.)
> Everything goes in and nothin' comes out.

14

Tar-Baby

I could cite a lot of reasons why I needed to sever my connection with
Operation Greylord. I was tired, I was frustrated, and I was frightened.

The bad guys had quickly discovered our phone taps, and they
knew Victor was a federal agent. Finally, we lost out on the contrived
cases. It was easy to make the decision to get out.

However, getting out was not as simple as making the decision. In
the process, I kept thinking about the Tar-Baby in the Uncle Remus
story—Brer Rabbit tricked Brer Fox into hitting the Tar-Baby, then
Brer Fox found he could not escape from the Tar-Baby. My version of
the story was not nearly as humorous as the original.

I had given the FBI and the U.S. attorney's office notice that I would
be quitting as of May 1. The U.S. attorney's office called several
meetings in my room to discuss the matter. They wanted me to stay
on, but I wasn't sure what they wanted me to do. When I told them
that, the only reply I got was, "We're on hold at the moment."

When they continued to press for an answer as to why I didn't want
to stay, I finally told them that I thought we had blown it all when the
FBI agents got caught with their pants down at Water Tower Place.

Around April 10, I wrote my boss, Robert Chase, chief judge of the
First Judicial Circuit, requesting that I be relieved of my Chicago
assignments after May 1. Judge Chase had been lukewarm to this
whole project from the start. I think he was afraid of repercussions
from the administrative office of the Illinois Supreme Court.

145

Since I had put in substantially more time than is normally required of an associate (six weeks a year), and because our circuit had more time accumulated for the first half of the year than was required, I didn't think I would have any trouble being relieved.

But the administrative office of the Illinois Supreme Court refused to allow me to go home early. As a matter of fact, they indicated that if I didn't continue going to Chicago I might be held in contempt of court and jailed. Great! I'd be the first Greylord judge to go to prison.

A year earlier I might have complied with their orders. But now circumventing the rules had become a way of life. I simply returned home, called in sick, and went to see my doctor. I explained to him that I wasn't sleeping, that I had lost twenty pounds, and that I thought I was about to have a nervous breakdown.

The doctor prescribed some sleeping pills and suggested that I rest for a few weeks. While the administrative office fumed, I relaxed at home with the horses. I started to catch up on sleep and spent quality time with my family and friends. I felt like a new man—like a great burden had been lifted.

But I still couldn't relax completely. At least not yet. For the next year and a half, I would be waiting and wondering. Waiting for the trials to start, and wondering, in the meantime, whether my involvement would be prematurely disclosed. I didn't have any idea how much longer it would take before the project became public, and I was restless to get it over with so I could get on with my life.

There were some tense times, too, during that period. In the late summer I was confronted by a man with a gun. He intended to kill me and himself because of a sentence I had imposed upon his son. I remember thinking during the encounter how ironic it would be that my demise had nothing to do with Greylord.

Then Ira showed up on two occasions. The first time he came to the house unannounced and left a note on my door. I didn't know what he wanted or why he was there, so I avoided him.

The second time, he called ahead. He said he wanted to visit his cousin who was incarcerated at the penitentiary in Marion. Marion Federal Penitentiary is the replacement for Alcatraz. Besides housing the world's most dangerous criminals "behind the wall," it contains a camp, which Ira wanted to get in to take a look at.

Because Ira was a policeman, I was able to arrange for him to visit his cousin at the camp on relatively short notice. Of course I couldn't get any help from the U.S. attorney's office and had to do it all on my own.

Ira and his wife came by the evening before, and Kathy and I went out dancing with them. The next morning, I took Ira to the prison. As usual, I was wearing a body recorder and was concerned about whether or not it would be detected when we entered the prison campgrounds. I didn't intend to go inside, but I had to go through the gate to drop off Ira.

Everything went well. I recorded Ira's reasons for going to the camp and his reaction to it.

Ira explained he thought he was in trouble in connection with the parking ticket scam and that he might have to do some time. His connections indicated that he could pick his camp. Apparently he was going around and checking to see which facility he liked the best.

After the visit, he indicated he liked the federal prison at Marion.

"It's a piece of cake—I could do the time standing on my head there," he told me.

It was like taking a kid to look at colleges. Ira told me then that he was the only adult male in his family that he knew about who hadn't gone to prison.

By the spring of 1983, we were talking about "flipping" Ira. I had convinced Dan Webb, who in turn had convinced the rest of the group, that Ira was a valuable source. I didn't know if we could get him to cooperate, but I thought it might be worth the effort.

That spring, we made arrangements for me to spend some time with Ira. I took him to a Cubs ballgame and afterwards went along while he paid off a judge on behalf of Bert Pillar. I tried to convince the federal people that I should talk to Ira about flipping during that trip. They thought it was too risky and I couldn't convince them otherwise.

But by that summer, however, they decided to make the approach. They asked Ira to come in and talk with them off the record.

Ira was told he was facing twenty years and a loss of his pension if he didn't cooperate. Ira calmly asked the investigator, "What have you got on me?"

"We've had a tap on your phone, a pin register on the phone that tells us who you were talking to, Victor Ries is an undercover agent, and Judge Lockwood has been wired for the last three years," the investigator explained.

"My God. What did you have on Lockwood?" Ira asked.

At the end of the interview, Ira asked for time to think about things. What he really needed was time on the street to guarantee his future.

In Chicago, custom dictates that the man who is caught serves his sentence, and all the people he does not identify to the investigating authorities pay his family's expenses while he's in jail.

I don't know if Ira was successful in getting his sponsors set up to pay the load. I'm sure he tried.

Instead of cooperating, Ira blew the whistle on Greylord. The next thing I knew, I was reading about the undercover operation, "as yet unnamed," in the *Chicago Tribune*. When I saw the story, I knew Ira had rejected any offers of leniency. The system had conditioned him to accept the penalties on behalf of the crooked judges.

I had expected him to make the choice he made, but I hated it when he did. He didn't even like the people he was protecting. But they had chosen to trust him, and he was not about to breach that trust.

His mistake was that he had trusted me.

15

The Trials and Tribulations

It seemed to take a long time for the initial Greylord cases to be filed. But once they were filed, things began to fall into place.

Unexpectedly, at the last moment, Richard LeFevour's cousin Jimmy decided to cooperate. Jimmy had served as Judge LeFevour's whipping boy for years, and I guess he decided there was no reason to protect the judge.

Jimmy's decision came after he was indicted, using evidence obtained through telephone conversations with Ira. Apparently Jimmy went to LeFevour for help, and LeFevour refused to see him. He was afraid that Jimmy might be wired.

The first judge to be tried was John M. Murphy. When Judge Murphy came to trial, Jimmy laid out the whole sordid scheme of rent, fines, and the Hustler's Club—a group of lawyers who paid LeFevour for the privilege of handling cases. Judge LeFevour, who had vehemently denied these allegations during the trial, promptly resigned when Judge Murphy was convicted.

When Judge LeFevour stepped down, I knew the whole project had been worth everything I had endured.

In order to avoid any appearance of political motivation, Webb waited until after the election, in the fall of 1984, to file the grand jury indictment charging Judge Richard F. LeFevour with seventy-one separate federal violations. The state could no longer ignore the problem at this point. The second most powerful judge in Cook County had been caught in the act—he was corrupt.

149

Operation Greylord got a big boost when Webb himself success-fully tried and convicted Judge Murphy. In fact, everything went so well that the public seemed to think these would be easy cases. This false perception was shattered during the trial of Judge John Laurie.

During the Laurie trial, Terry Hake—a former state's attorney turned undercover FBI agent—testified that he had never actually put any money in Judge Laurie's hand. He had given it to one of the Trunzo brothers, and then he had received favorable decisions from Judge Laurie. Patrolman Trunzo testified that he, in fact, had placed the money at designated places within the judge's office—in his coat or in a desk drawer.

The jury listened to a tape in which Hake and Judge Laurie dis-cussed a case. The judge advised Hake that if he wanted to get his client off, he had better advise his client to lie. Then Judge Laurie laughed.

Laurie, an affable, nice-looking man, testified on his own behalf. He claimed that he had never received money from patrolman Trunzo or anyone else. He did confess that he was, perhaps, an easy judge because he always resolved any doubt in favor of the defendant. Finally, he testified that he had told Terry Hake to advise his client to lie—but he was just kidding. He pointed out that he had laughed after he made the remark.

The jury found Judge Laurie not guilty.

There were two defendants about whom I had the most direct knowledge regarding criminal violations—Tommie and Ira. Tommie had fled to Greece, so I had to be concerned only with Ira. His trial began before Judge Laurie's had ended. Before I took the stand, the jury in Judge Laurie's case returned a verdict of "not guilty."

I was glad then that Assistant U.S. Attorney John Newman had been assigned to put Ira's case together. I was sure he would leave no holes through which the defendant could escape. Newman was an experienced trial attorney—intelligent, dedicated, and competent—who in ten years with the U.S. attorney's office had never lost a case. He was thorough to the point of being tedious. That was what made him good. It is usually the detail man who wins the marginal cases in court, not the flamboyant charmer who ends up on the nighttime talk shows.

Newman first called me about eight months before Ira's trial, to tell me he had been assigned to the case. He apologized when he asked me to listen to all the tapes again. He wanted me to compare them with the transcript that had been prepared. Newman said he was depressed that the system had gotten so bad before anyone did anything about it. He was also upset it had been an outsider, not a former U.S. attorney or a reputable Chicago attorney, who had blown the whistle. I didn't share those feelings.

Listening to the tapes was a task I dreaded. I felt guilty about abusing Ira's confidence. Undercover work was something I just wasn't cut out to do. I didn't have the right kind of personality and got too intimately involved with the targets.

However, hearing those tapes turned out to be therapeutic. We spent five or six days—very long days in which Newman acted as if he resented taking even a half-hour break for lunch—listening to Ira explain his philosophy of life. Suddenly, I saw him as he really was—a ruthless and dangerous individual. He was a sociopath who would rather play outside the rules of society than within them, and he didn't care who got hurt. His attitude toward the numerous people whom he victimized was, "fuck 'em!"

I don't know why I had never sensed how bad Ira really was. He had revealed himself to me slowly, and by the time he began to share his distorted views of life, I was so consumed with guilt about abusing his confidence that I refused to judge him too harshly. I ignored or forgot about all the people in the system he had hurt.

By the time I finished reviewing the tapes, I no longer doubted it had been appropriate for me to record our conversations. I didn't like what Ira had done. I didn't like what I had done to him, either. But it had been necessary.

When I took the stand in Ira's case, he glared at me for perhaps half an hour. After that, he remained a casual observer. I was surprised at how calm he looked.

Ira's lawyer, Joe Roddy, is the attorney for the Police Benevolent Association in Chicago, and I wouldn't consider him an experienced trial lawyer. He seemed to be a nice fellow who was uncomfortable about asking the tough questions.

The defense Roddy suggested to the jury was that Ira had been "puffing" about all the things he had done—or could do. He explained that Ira was just spinning stories for an "ignorant hillbilly judge from downstate." None of those stories was true.

Apparently, Roddy felt he might have offended some members of the jury by calling me an "ignorant hillbilly" in his opening statement. During his cross examination, he tried to rectify the potential problem.

> RODDY: Just so we are off on the right foot, I have never used the word "ignorant," sir. I used the word "innocent."
> LOCKWOOD: It is the second word that causes some concern.

Roddy blushed. I smiled. The jury laughed.

It was Roddy's position that Ira was conning me about all his big, important friends. In order to illustrate to the jury that I had been foolish to believe Ira, he read portions of the recorded transcripts of our conversations.

Unfortunately, Roddy had agreed to delete the names of important people during the trial so they would not be embarrassed unnecessarily. But, without those names, Roddy's cross examination made little sense. The following is a verbatim portion of the transcript.

> RODDY: Does he not say: You know blank's there and blank, and blank's a personal friend of mine. I broke him in, and blank is a top outfit guy. I mean, shit, I got all the clout out there you need, and nobody has got more clout.
> You say: Where is it?
> He says: It's out in Maywood, I got all the blank clout you need. Blank's boss is out there, he is from the First Ward. That's his brother-in-law, blank, and blank's married to blank, who is a personal friend of mine for years, you know, the Senator.
> Then you say: Yes.
> He says: Well, as long as we can't do nothing here, blank, it will get out of here.
> Yeah, yeah, I agree.
> Is that correct?
> LOCKWOOD: Yes.

Apparently, the jury was not confused by the cross examination. They quickly returned a verdict of guilty on all thirteen counts. Ira was sentenced to seven years in the penitentiary.

By the time of Ira's trial, I was no longer a judge. I had resigned about four months earlier.

I could have remained a judge after my exposure with Greylord. I had a great deal of local support from downstate judges, and Bill Lewis, the new chief judge, promised that he would send other people to Chicago in my place. I declined his generous offer because I didn't want other people to serve for me—I didn't want downstate judges to have to go at all. And if I were to remain on the bench, I felt I should carry my share of the load.

I was disillusioned with the system and with the people in positions of authority. I didn't want to remain a part of it. Besides, I had had enough of sitting on the passive side of the bench. The experience I gained as a judge was invaluable, but I wanted to get back to work as a trial lawyer. Giving up the bench was the right decision and I'm happier for it. I have never regretted my action.

After Ira's case was concluded, my life resumed some semblance of normalcy. With the exception of two more cases and a few public speaking engagements, I had little more to do with Operation Greylord. It has now been five years since my participation. The statute of limitations has run its course. Although I may be formally finished with the project, it continues to occupy my mind. It probably always will. The operation continues to grind on—trial after trial. Someday perhaps most of the rotten apples will be gone. I hope so.

At first, I didn't expect many people would be convicted as a result of the Greylord investigation. The result has been surprising—and gratifying. As the writing of this book is concluded, the number of persons who have either pled guilty or been convicted approaches seventy. The conviction that meant most to me was that of Judge Richard LeFevour—the kingpin of the whole corrupt operation.

Dan Webb had resigned prior to the LeFevour trial to go into private practice. It is difficult to keep good people in relatively low-paying positions for long. I was concerned about whether his successor would push the Greylord cases as Webb would have done. I was also concerned about who was going to try LeFevour.

I knew Dan Reidy was geared up for the LeFevour case, but I also knew that LeFevour planned to hire Pat Tuite as his trial attorney. Tuite was a good, solid criminal defense lawyer—and had successfully defended Judge Laurie. While I had confidence in Reidy, I was relieved when I learned that Dan Webb would come back to try LeFevour.

If I could somehow have remained inconspicuous, I would have attended the LeFevour trial. Apparently, it was quite a contest.

The first day, in open court, LeFevour chastised the federal judge for one of his prior rulings. The judge, who was relatively new to the federal bench, was a former associate circuit judge in the state court system. I wondered whether he had worked in traffic court under LeFevour and whether he might somehow be intimidated by, or perhaps sympathetic to, LeFevour.

Apparently he was not.

He had his hands full, nevertheless. The contest between Tuite and Webb was vigorous. At one point, the federal judge found it necessary to hold Tuite in contempt of court and fine him for his remarks.

The real contest—the one that everyone wanted to see—was the confrontation between Webb and LeFevour. Everyone anticipated that LeFevour would have to testify in his own behalf. Webb, who is noted for his skillful cross-examinations, was gearing up for a lengthy exchange.

It never occurred.

Tuite recognized that LeFevour could not take the stand successfully. Apparently, he didn't want Webb opening any more holes in the defense than had already been established. From that point in the trial, when LeFevour indicated that he would not testify, he lost his self-assurance. LeFevour suddenly looked his age—fifty-three—and then some.

Reidy and Webb methodically built their case against LeFevour. It was a tedious and difficult task. Among other things, they disclosed to the jury that the defendant could not justify, on his salary, his investments and his substantial expenditures over the past several years.

On the other side, Tuite's defense was to show the jury that LeFevour was a nice man, with a nice family, who enjoyed the respect of a large segment of the community. LeFevour tried to claim that he got all the money from personal loans from friends and relatives.

The jury was not impressed. They convicted Judge LeFevour on all fifty-nine counts.

I considered the sentence—twelve years—to be somewhat light in the LeFevour case. However, the conviction was the most important thing.

It sent a clear message to people throughout the system that no one was big enough or powerful enough to flaunt the laws of our nation and ignore the possibility of criminal prosecution.

During the Laurie trial, Judge Harry Comerford announced that he was creating a blue ribbon commission to study the problem of judicial corruption in the Chicago courts and to take steps to correct it. I wondered at the time whether the state was finally assuming some of its responsibility or whether Judge Comerford's commission was just a ploy to placate the news media. I didn't expect much would be done. Blue ribbon commissions in the past have been a dime a dozen.

Since the group had no money and no investigative powers, I thought it was just a paper tiger. But Judge Comerford put some very good people on the commission. They obtained independent funding so they did not have to answer to anyone. I think that step was most important.

The director, Peter Manikas, has pushed hard to find constructive ways for the legal profession to police itself. He believes, as I do, that the legal profession has an obligation to deal with the problems of corruption and incompetence in a firm, realistic, and effective fashion. It is not an easy task.

I have been surprised and sincerely impressed with the work the commission has been able to accomplish thus far. It seems to be confronting the problems of professional misconduct in a systematic fashion, not just applying cosmetics or piecing together a patchwork solution. This is the first time this has been done. Perhaps some solutions will be found. That, in the long run, might be the most significant aspect of Greylord.

Chicago's dark side has an amazing resiliency. Despite the disclosure of Bert Pillar's role in disposing of damaging court documents, he remains in a very important appointive city office. Gino Superchi now holds a prestigious elected office within state government.

I could be cynical and say, "And so it goes." But I won't say that. Not yet, at least.

I was recently in Chicago talking to the U.S. attorney's office about a couple of other Greylord cases. I knew Ira had been cooperating in order to lessen his sentence. I also knew that he had been spending time in the U.S. attorney's office. The various assistants there had refused to allow me to talk to him directly. They were afraid of his reaction.

By accident, I walked into the bathroom as Ira was walking out. He looked cold and controlled.

I asked, "How's it going?"

He responded, "Great—thanks to you." It was a sarcastic remark, but at least, so far, he was controlling his hostility.

I wonder how he'll be when he gets out.

From a personal standpoint, Greylord allowed me to be myself. I don't worry anymore about whether I'm a success or a failure. It is no longer important. Because of that I'm glad I had the experience. I am much happier now, and I no longer think my death is imminent.

A high school teacher said to me, not long ago, that it was a great opportunity to be allowed to participate in Operation Greylord. He was right. I believe that the Jimmy Hoffa case, Watergate, Abscam, and Operation Greylord were all necessary and appropriate steps in re-establishing the very basic principle that, in this country, no person or group—regardless of power and prestige—is above the law.

While I feel fortunate that I got to see history in the making, and to be a part of it, I am even luckier to have had the chance to pay back something I owed. Perhaps it's because I didn't serve in Vietnam or because I've had more opportunities than some, but I never felt as if I had "paid for my raisin'."

I haven't satisfied that debt yet, but I feel more comfortable about it.

Appendix

Appendix
Operation Greylord Convictions as of 1988

Convicted Judges

Defendant	Position	Conviction	Sentence
John J. Devine 83 CR 981	Associate Judge	Convicted Oct. 8, 1984 on one racketeering/ conspiracy count, 25 extortion counts and 21 mail fraud counts.	15 years prison
Martin F. Hogan 85 CR 813	Former Associate Judge	Convicted Aug. 29, 1988 on one racketeering/ bribery count, one racketeering/ conspiracy count and three tax counts.*	(Sentencing pending)
Reginald J. Holzer 85 CR 287	Circuit Judge	Convicted Feb. 18, 1986 on one racketeering/ bribery count, three extortion counts and 23 mail fraud counts. Racketeering/ bribery and mail fraud convictions reversed by the Seventh Circuit Court of Appeals on February 19, 1988.	Resentenced to 13 years prison

Source: Special Commission on the Administration of Justice in Cook County, Final Report, 1988.

*"Tax counts," unless otherwise indicated, refer to the felony charge of filing false income tax statements.

Convicted Judges (Cont'd.)

Defendant	Position	Conviction	Sentence
Richard F. LeFevour 84 CR 837	Presiding Judge— First Municipal District	Convicted July 13, 1985 on one racketeering/ bribery count, 53 mail fraud counts and five tax counts.	12 years prison
John H. McCollom 86 CR 410-11	Circuit Judge	Pleaded guilty May 1, 1987 to eight racketeering/ conspiracy counts and two tax counts.	11 years prison, 5 years probation
Michael E. McNulty 87 CR 963	Former Associate Judge	Pleaded guilty Dec. 16, 1987 to three tax counts.	3 years prison, $15,000 fine, 3 years probation, 600 hours community service
John M. Murphy 83 CR 979	Associate Judge	Convicted June 14, 1984 on one racketeering/ conspiracy count, seven extortion counts and 16 mail fraud counts.	10 years prison, 5 years probation
Wayne W. Olson 83 CR 978	Circuit Judge	Pleaded guilty July 18, 1985 to one racketeering/ bribery count, one extortion count and one mail fraud count.	12 years prison, $35,000 fine, 5 years probation

Convicted Judges (Cont'd.)

Defendant	Position	Conviction	Sentence
John F. Reynolds 85 CR 812	Circuit Judge	Convicted May 7, 1986 on one racketeering/ bribery count, one racketeering/ conspiracy count, six extortion counts, 25 mail fraud counts and three tax counts.	10 years prison, $33,000 fine
		Pleaded guilty April 8, 1988 to two perjury counts.	2 years prison, 2 years probation
Roger E. Seaman 87 CR 928	Former Associate Judge	Pleaded guilty Dec. 16, 1987 to two mail fraud counts and one tax count.	(Sentencing pending)
Raymond C. Sodini 85 CR 813	Circuit Judge	Pleaded guilty Jan. 20, 1987 to one racketeering/ conspiracy count and one tax count.	8 years prison, 5 years probation, 750 hours community service

Convicted Attorneys

Defendant	Position	Conviction	Sentence
Hugo Arquillo 87 CR 967	Attorney	Pleaded guilty Dec. 16, 1987 to two tax counts*	2 months work release, $1,300 fine, 3 years probation, 200 hours community service.
Lee Barnett 85 CR 813	Attorney	Pleaded guilty Jan. 15, 1987 to one racketeering/ conspiracy count and one mail fraud count.	6 months prison, 2 years probation
Lebert D. Bastianoni 87 CR 214	Attorney	Pleaded guilty July 6, 1987 to two tax counts.	30 days work release, $5,000 fine, 4 years probation, 500 hours community service, ordered to pay back taxes and penalties
Harlan Becker 84 CR 813	Attorney	Convicted Feb. 17, 1987 on two tax counts. Pleaded guilty Nov. 6, 1987 to one racketeering/ conspiracy count and one racketeering/ bribery count.	6 years prison, $60,000 fine, 5 years probation, ordered to pay $63,000 in back taxes and penalties
Jerry B. Berliant 84 CR 834	Attorney	Pleaded guilty April 15, 1985 to three tax counts.	20 weekends in jail, 3 years probation
Neal Birnbaum 85 CR 813	Attorney	Pleaded guilty Oct. 14, 1987 to one racketeering/ conspiracy count, one racketeering/ bribery count and one mail fraud count.	(Sentencing pending)

*"Tax counts," unless otherwise indicated, refer to the felony charge of filing false income tax statements.

Convicted Attorneys (Cont'd.)

Defendant	Position	Conviction	Sentence
Dale Boton 88 CR 216	Attorney	Pleaded guilty Mar. 23, 1988 to four misdemeanor tax counts for failure to file income tax returns.	90 days work release, 3 years probation, 300 hours community service
Howard M. Brandstein 85 CR 813	Attorney	Pleaded guilty Sept. 19, 1986 to one racketeering/ conspiracy count and one tax count.	1 year and one day prison, $56,000 forfeiture, 5 years probation, 200 hours community service
Houston Burnside 85 CR 813	Attorney	Pleaded guilty June 5, 1985 to three tax counts.	30 weekends in prison, $3,000 fine, 3 years probation
Bruce L. Campbell, Jr. 86 CR 410	Attorney	Pleaded guilty Feb. 4, 1987 to one racketeering/ bribery count and one tax count.	1 year prison, 6 months of which is work release; 5 years probation
James I. Canoff 84 CR 249	Ass't Corporation Counsel	Pleaded guilty April 17, 1984 to one racketeering/ bribery count, 18 mail fraud counts and one obstruction of justice count.	6 months work release, 300 hours community service, $5,000 restitution to the City of Chicago
James J. Costello 83 CR 978	Attorney	Pleaded guilty July 18, 1985 to one racketeering/ bribery count and one mail fraud count.	8 years prison, $100 fine, 5 years probation

Convicted Attorneys (Cont'd.)

Defendant	Position	Conviction	Sentence
Robert Daniels 85 CR 813	Attorney	Convicted Feb. 17, 1987 on two tax counts. Pending trial on one racketeering/ bribery count and one racketeering/ conspiracy count.	6 years prison
Vincent E. Davino 85 CR 813	Attorney	Pleaded guilty Jan. 16, 1987 to one racketeering/ conspiracy count and one mail fraud count.	4 years prison, 5 years probation, 500 hours community service
Thomas F. DelBeccaro 85 CR 812	Attorney	Pleaded guilty April 11, 1986 to two mail fraud counts.	90 days in prison, later revoked; $1,000 fine; 5 years probation
Thurman Gardner 84 CR 836	Attorney	Pleaded guilty April 1, 1985 to four tax counts.	6 months prison, 3 years probation, 750 hours community service
Richard H. Goldstein 86 CR 410	Attorney	Pleaded guilty Feb. 4, 1987 to one racketeering/ conspiracy count and one tax count.	1 year prison, 6 months of which is work release; 5 years probation; 400 hours community service
Alphonse C. Gonzales 84 CR 248	Attorney	Pleaded guilty June 25, 1986 to two tax counts and on July 8, 1986 to one extortion count.	3 years prison, later reduced to 1 year; $2,000 fine; 5 years probation
William H. Kampenga 88 CR 215	Attorney	Pleaded guilty Mar. 23, 1988 to two tax counts.	(Sentencing pending)

Convicted Attorneys (Cont'd.)

Defendant	Position	Conviction	Sentence
Melvin Kanter 86 CR 410-12	Attorney	Pleaded guilty Dec. 17, 1986 to one racketeering/ bribery count.	90 days work release, $25,000 fine, 5 years probation, 400 hours community service
Edward Kaplan 84 CR 244	Attorney	Pleaded guilty Jan. 28, 1985 to three tax counts.	2 years prison, 5 years probation
Paul G. Kulerski 86 CR 410	Attorney	Pleaded guilty March 18, 1985 to two tax counts.	3 months prison, 5 years probation, 400 hours community service
Bernard N. Mann 86 CR 410	Attorney	Pleaded guilty Feb. 25, 1987 to one racketeering/ bribery count and one tax count.	6 months prison, $25,000 fine, 5 years probation, 400 hours community service
Joseph E. McDermott 86 CR 410-11	Attorney	Pleaded guilty Dec. 10, 1986 to one racketeering/ bribery count and one tax count.	1 year and one day prison, $30,000 fine, 5 years probation
Ralph E. Meczyk 87 CR 214	Attorney	Pleaded guilty July 6, 1987 to two tax counts.	30 days work release, $5,000 fine, 4 years probation, 500 hours community service, ordered to pay back taxes and penalties
Jay I. Messinger 83 CR 979	Attorney	Convicted May 8, 1986 on one mail fraud count.	2 years prison, $1,000 fine

Convicted Attorneys (Cont'd.)

Defendant	Position	Conviction	Sentence
James E. Noland 86 CR 410	Attorney	Pleaded guilty March 27, 1987 to one racketeering/ bribery count and one tax count.	15 months prison, $15,000 fine, 5 years probation, 400 hours community service
Edward E. Nydam 85 CR 812	Attorney	Pleaded guilty April 29, 1985 to two tax counts and on Feb. 25, 1986 to one mail fraud count.	6 months prison, 5 years probation (on tax counts only)
James L. Oakey 85 CR 813	Attorney, Former Associate Judge	Convicted May 15, 1987 on two tax counts. Pending trial on one racketeering/ bribery count and one racketeering/ conspiracy count.	18 months prison, $5,000 fine, 5 years probation, ordered to pay back taxes and penalties
Cary N. Polikoff 87 CR 928	Attorney	Pleaded guilty Aug. 22, 1988 to two mail fraud counts.	(Sentencing pending)
William F. Reilly 86 CR 410	Attorney	Pleaded guilty March 27, 1987 to one racketeering/ bribery count and one tax count.	14 months prison, $5,000 fine, 5 years probation, 400 hours community service
Mark Rosenbloom 87 CR 965	Attorney	Pleaded guilty March 11, 1988 to two tax counts.	2 years probation, 300 hours community service
Bruce Roth 85 CR 763	Attorney	Convicted Aug. 24, 1987 on two extortion counts, one racketeering/ bribery count and one racketeering/ conspiracy count.	10 years prison, 5 years probation

Convicted Attorneys (Cont'd.)

Defendant	Position	Conviction	Sentence
Martin Schachter 84 CR 242	Attorney	Pleaded guilty July 5, 1984 to one mail fraud count.	4 years probation
R. Frederic Solomon 85 CR 814	Attorney	Pleaded guilty April 8, 1986 to four tax counts.	2½ years prison, 5 years probation
Dean S. Wolfson 83 CR 976	Attorney	Pleaded guilty Jan. 25, 1985 to one racketeering/ bribery count and three mail fraud counts.	7½ years prison, $3,000 fine, 5 years probation
Cyrus Yonan, Jr. 84 CR 246	Attorney	Pleaded guilty May 14, 1987 to one racketeering/ bribery count and two tax counts.	1 year and one day prison, $15,000 fine, 3 years probation, 400 hours community service, ordered to pay $12,300 in back taxes and penalties
Arthur Zimmerman 87 CR 966	Attorney	Pleaded guilty Dec. 22, 1987 to two tax counts.	3 years prison, $10,000 fine, 3 years probation, 300 hours community service

Convicted Court Personnel

Defendant	Position	Conviction	Sentence
Gaetano Bianco 87 CR 690	Deputy Sheriff	Pleaded guilty to one misdemeanor count for civil rights violation.	(No information available; court file sealed.)
Ira J. Blackwood 83 CR 977	Police Officer	Convicted Aug. 10, 1984 on one racketeering/ bribery count and ten extortion counts.	7 years prison, $20,000 fine, 5 years probation
Harold J. Conn 83 CR 983	Deputy Clerk	Convicted March 15, 1984 of one racketeering/ bribery count and nine extortion counts.	6 years prison, $2,000 fine, 5 years probation
James F. Hegarty 85 CR 813	Police Officer	Pleaded guilty Feb. 28, 1986 to one tax count.*	3 years probation, 300 hours community service
Leopoldo Hernandez 85 CR 432	Deputy Sheriff	Pleaded guilty July 31, 1985 to one extortion count.	6 months work release, 5 years probation, 500 hours community service
Paul B. Hutson 85 CR 813	Deputy Sheriff	Pleaded guilty Feb. 25, 1986 to one misdemeanor tax count for failure to file income tax returns.	60 days work release, 5 years probation
Alan Kaye 83 CR 980	Deputy Sheriff	Convicted March 1, 1985 of official misconduct, theft, bribery and intimidation counts (in state court).	5 years (state prison)

*"Tax counts," unless otherwise indicated, refer to the felony charge of filing false income tax statements.

Convicted Court Personnel (Cont'd.)

Defendant	Position	Conviction	Sentence
Jerome R. Kohn 85 CR 813	Deputy Sheriff	Pleaded guilty Jan. 26, 1987 to one racketeering/ conspiracy count and one tax count.	18 months prison, $10,000 fine, 5 years probation
Nick La Palombella 85 CR 813	Deputy Clerk	Pleaded guilty Feb. 25, 1986 to one tax count.	60 days work release, 5 years probation
James R. LeFevour 84 CR 837	Police Officer	Pleaded guilty Dec. 4, 1984 to three tax counts.	30 months prison
Henry F. Lemanski 88 CR 322	Deputy Clerk	Pleaded guilty Aug. 30, 1988 to two obstruction of justice counts.	(Sentencing pending)
Arthur W. McCauslin 84 CR 837	Police Officer	Pleaded guilty Dec. 4, 1984 to two tax counts.	18 months prison
Lawrence E. McLain 84 CR 837	Police Officer	Pleaded guilty Dec. 4, 1984 to two tax counts.	15 months prison
Frank L. Mirabella 85 CR 813	Deputy Sheriff	Pleaded guilty Sept. 19, 1986 to two racketeering/ bribery counts and one tax count.	7 months prison, $15,000 fine, 5 years probation, 300 hours community service
Lucious Robinson 88 CR 219	Deputy Sheriff	Pleaded guilty June 27, 1988 to one extortion count.	3 years prison, $3,000 fine
Steve Ruben 85 CR 813	Deputy Sheriff	Pleaded guilty Feb. 25, 1986 to one tax count.	(Sentencing pending)

Convicted Court Personnel (Cont'd.)

Defendant	Position	Conviction	Sentence
Patrick J. Ryan 85 CR 813	Deputy Sheriff	Pleaded guilty Feb. 25, 1986 to one racketeering/ bribery count and one tax count.	60 days work release, 5 years probation
James V. Trunzo 84 CR 245	Police Officer	Pleaded guilty Sept. 5, 1984 to two tax counts.	1 year prison, $10,000 fine, 3 years probation
Joseph Trunzo 84 CR 245	Police Officer	Pleaded guilty Sept. 5, 1984 to two tax counts.	1 year prison, $10,000 fine, 3 years probation
Ernest Worsek 85 CR 288	Receiver	Pleaded guilty Oct. 22, 1985 to one mail fraud count and one misdemeanor tax count for failure to file income tax returns.	6 months prison
Nick Yokas 85 CR 813	Deputy Sheriff	Pleaded guilty Feb 25, 1986 to one tax count.	60 days work release, 5 years probation

Brocton Lockwood grew up on his grandfather's farm near Carbondale, Illinois. While attending Oberlin College he worked for a local police department and became interested in the legal system. After college he attended Vanderbilt University and worked part time for the United States attorney's office. In 1969 he returned to his hometown to enter private practice as a trial attorney. Between 1972 and 1978 he taught constitutional law courses at Southern Illinois University. In 1978 he was appointed as an associate circuit judge, a position he held until 1983. He has now returned to the private practice of law, again as a trial lawyer.

An Oklahoma native, Harlan H. Mendenhall has been a part of the media scene since 1937 when he graduated from the University of Oklahoma. His first job was as a reporter for the *Daily Oklahoman*. In the field of radio, he was a writer for the CBS series, "Gang Busters." A prolific true-crime magazine writer, he wrote for Dell, Fawcett, and Triangle publications. During World War II, Mendenhall served as a propaganda writer/motion picture cameraman for the Army Air Corps. He ended his television career as a news writer for ABC in Los Angeles. In 1967, he changed careers and began to teach creative writing and reporting at Southern Illinois University. In 1986 Mendenhall retired after being voted "Great Teacher of the Year" by the Southern Illinois University Alumni Association.